THE MIS-EDUCATION
OF THE NEGRO

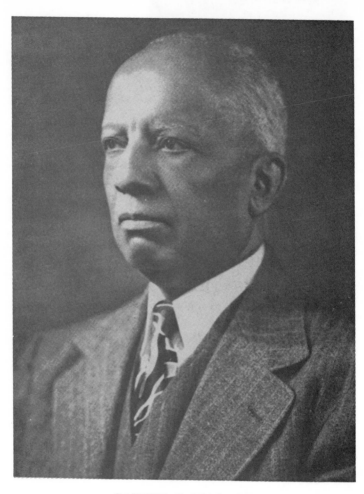

CARTER G. WOODSON
1875 - 1950
HISTORIAN, AUTHOR, EDUCATOR

THE MIS-EDUCATION
OF THE NEGRO

BY

CARTER GODWIN WOODSON

Edited with an Introduction by Charles H. Wesley
and Thelma D. Perry

THE ASSOCIATED PUBLISHERS, INC.
1407 14th Street, N.W.
Washington, D.C. 20005

INTRODUCTION

Considerable time has passed since the first printing of this volume, but it is significant that it has meaning and direct implications for today's consideration. While it does not relate exclusively to Black History it does emphasize its instruction, research and writing. In substance Carter Woodson has produced a definitive and constructive critique of the educational system, with special reference to its blighting effects on the Negro; and the term he used, *Mis-education,* was the most apt and descriptive word available. It is still, in 1969, equally as relevant and expressive. Now, however, it is loudly articulated by many voices of Whites as well as Blacks, who likewise challenge the system.

The most imperative and crucial element in Woodson's concept of *mis-education* hinged on the education system's failure to present authentic Negro History in schools and the bitter knowledge that there was a scarcity of literature available for such a purpose, because most history books gave little or no space to the black man's presence in America. Some of them contained casual references to Negroes but these generally depicted them in menial, subordinate roles, more or less sub-human. Such books stressed their good fortune at having been exposed, through slavery, to the higher (white man's) civilization. There were included derogatory statements relating to the primitive, heathenish quality of the African background, but nothing denoting skills, abilities, contributions or potential in the image of the Blacks, in Africa or America. Woodson considered this state of affairs deplorable, an American tragedy, dooming the Negro to a brain-washed acceptance of the inferior role assigned to him by the dominant race, and absorbed by him through his schooling.

Moreover, the neglect of Afro-American History and distortion of the facts concerning Negroes in most history books, deprived the black child and his whole race of a heritage, and relegated him to nothingness and nobodyness. This was Woodson's conviction as he stated it in this book and as he lived by it. In his Annual Report of the Association for the Study of Negro Life and History for the year ending June 30, 1933, the publication period of *Mis-Education,* he stated:

> Regarding the Negro race as a factor in world culture rather than as an element in a sequestered sphere, the Director (Woodson) has recently made two trips to Europe to extend the study of the notice taken of Negroes by European authors and artists, and to

engage a larger number of Europeans and Africans
in the study of the past of the Negro.[1]

Thus it is evident that the stress which Dr.
Woodson places on historical research, writing,
and teaching in this volume was not theoretical
jargon. It represented rather, a firm belief;
also a judgement of the available type of education that was so strongly oriented as to
warrant his complete and selfless dedication to
its betterment. This devotion became a crusade
which, in the above instance, carried him to
Europe in an effort to open new avenues for
recreating and writing of the black man's past.
This was in line with his basic charges against
the omission by most historians of such an
important part of history.

Mis-Education criticizes the system, and ex-
plains the vicious circle that results from *mis-
educated* individuals graduating, then proceed-
ing to teach and *mis-educate* others. But the
book is by no means a study in negation. The
author goes to great lengths in tracing the
historical foundations of the problem, its development, and its influence on interpersonal
relations and historical scholarship. Numerous
other scholars now follow its example.

The youths of the race were Woodson's particular concern because he recognized that it

---

[1] Annual Report of the Director of the Association for the
Study of Negro Life and History, Incorporated, July 1, 1932
to June 30, 1933. Washington, D. C. p. 4

was with the boys and girls that *Mis-education* began, later crystallizing into deep-seated insecurities, intra-racial cleavages, and inter-racial antagonisms. All of these factors have been discussed over and over in the immediate past, by historians, sociologists, psychiatrists, and laymen, but Dr. Woodson, and a pitifully small number of others, had pointed the way a full generation earlier.

More so than most of his contemporaries did Woodson contribute because he gave up a prestigious educational career, including a school principalship in Washington, D.C., the position of Dean at both Howard University and West Virginia State College. He decided instead to devote his finances and energies to an association which would help to overcome the inadequacies of the system which promoted *mis-education*. This was not by any means his first book but the views expressed herein form a sort of core or center, to and from which his texts and other writings protrude and revert.

All of this scholar's researches and writings were designed to provide educational sustenance, to fill the void which existed by reason of neglect of Black Studies. As has been already observed, however, he was no mere theorist, he was an activist and a pragmatist. He knew that writing alone would be inadequate for the enormity of the need. Consequently he, with four others, founded The Association for the Study of Negro Life and History, established the *Journal of Negro History,* and concentrated mightily on the educational aspect of his program, trying to counteract the poison of *mis-education.* In regard to these efforts he reported:

> The calls on the Research Department for assistance to teachers and students have multiplied so as to make this phase of the work a heavy burden on a small staff. Instructors now taking up the study of the Negro require help in working out courses in this new field; and their students are urged to make frequent use of the Department by correspondence or visits to the home of the Association.[2]

That statement is just as relevant in today's situation as it was when Woodson made it! As a matter of fact it might be copied and used by the present Director of the Association and it would be true except that the demand for services has increased a thousand-fold. The study of the Black man is *still new* in this generation, but such advances as have been made are in large part due to the vision, insight, writings, and publishing of pioneers like Carter Woodson. Indeed his analyses and conclusions regarding the entire educational system and its unrelatedness to future needs of the students stand firm, on solid ground. They were extendable to the 1960's, and student attitudes and actions make it quite clear that the reasoning

---

[2] Annual Report, *ibid.,* July 1, 1929 to June 30, 1930. p. 4

and recommendations of *Mis-Education* constitute a convenient point of departure for the current reformation of educational institutions.

If Woodson had been content with merely writing his own articles and books his contribution would have been monumental, because his production was tremendous and his methodology was scientific. He, however, conceived of this historical vacuum in terms of such magnitude that no one historian could possibly do enough research and writing to seek the facts, organize and present them, and correct the false and distorted information which had been passed off for true history for many generations. Consequently he sought, encouraged, and published the works of other scholars who shared his convictions and his sense of urgency in the premises.

As one noteworthy example, Lawrence D. Reddick has an analytical article of forty pages in the *Journal of Negro History* entitled "Racial Attitudes in American History Textbooks of the South."[3] In line with Woodson's complaints this author pointed out that the average pupil received a picture of slavery which generally managed to justify it, to ex-

---

3 Lawrence D. Reddick, "Racial Attitudes in American History Books in the South." *The Journal of Negro History* Volume XIX No. 3, July, 1934 pp. 225-265

plain the climate and economic conditions which fastened it to the South, and to minimize the hardships for blacks by emphasizing their good nature and song-singing. The textbook authors stressed the fact that there had been no practical way to free southern slaves, and blamed the northern abolitionists for the hardening of southern attitudes.

There was virtually nothing in the textbooks he explored that referred to the role and development of the Negro in national life after Reconstruction. His activities in the wars and national defense were completely ignored, and illustrations for all periods were almost nonexistent. Thus this article, accepted, edited, and published by Woodson, in all respects bore out his grievance against *Mis-education,* and it went to the very heart of his thesis.

In the same issue of the *Journal of Negro History* another article reinforced his views from a different investigative angle. Thomas L. Dabney made a survey of Negro and white colleges to determine the ones which offered courses in Negro History and/or Literature, or Race Relations; the Negro public schools which offered Negro History and/or Negro Literature; and the enrollment figures for both colleges and pre-college students. He also explained the purposes and progress of Negro History Week, as well as the home study courses offered by the Association for the Study of

Negro Life and History, and its clubs in their states.[4]

Another respected educator, Dr. Horace Mann Bond, was strongly aware of the substantive character of Dr. Woodson's charges of *Mis-Education,* particularly with regard to the curriculum under which the southern Negro child studied. In that connection he wrote, "The activities of the Association for the Study of Negro Life and History may . . . be said to represent a Negro nationalism which is a reaction against the 'white' nationalism of the American people."[5]

Then, referring to the curriculum builders who took "for granted that white supremacy had to be maintained," Bond declared:

> The load of what appears to the present writer, and Dr. Woodson, as propaganda, was not so considered by the former writers of southern textbooks, nor is it today.[6]

Thus it is apparent that Dr. Bond was either influenced by or was in agreement with the mis-education ideas which constituted so vital a part of Dr. Woodson's entire theory of the unfavorable effect of the American educational system on black children.

---

[4] Thomas L. Dabney, "The Study of the Negro." *The Journal of Negro History ibid.,* pp. 265-307

[5] Horace Mann Bond, "The Curriculum and the Negro Child" *Journal of Negro Education* Volume IV No. 2, April, 1935. p. 163 ff.

[6] *ibid.*

Many of the investigations were concentrated on the Southland and that is understandable. The bulk of the Negro population then lived below the Mason-Dixon line where no blacks were admitted to the white schools or colleges, and the dual system of education was obviously and definitely designed to perpetuate the Negro-inferiority image of the slavery period. Dr. Woodson also condemned the North for discrimination. As one who had studied at northern universities, The University of Chicago, and Harvard University, where he received the Ph.D degree, his experiences and observations enabled him to make valid judgments about that section.

One of his intellectual contemporaries, another Harvard-trained scholar, W. E. B. Du-Bois, was especially outspoken on northern education for Negroes, believing with Woodson, that it propagandized and indoctrinated youth, draining them of self-confidence, self-respect, and self-knowledge.

In 1935 DuBois wrote:

> . . . race prejudice in the United States today is such that most Negroes cannot receive proper education in white institutions . . . many public school systems in the North where Negroes are admitted and tolerated but they are not educated; they are crucified . . . certain Northern universities where Negro students . . . cannot get fair recognition, either in classroom or on the campus, in dining hall or student activities, or in human common courtesy . . . at Harvard, Yale, and

Columbia, Negroes are admitted but not welcomed;
while in other institutions like Princeton they cannot
even enroll.[7]

In further development of his thesis that
Blacks needed special education, Dr. DuBois
made a point-blank statement with respect to a
constructive means of overcoming the *mis-
education* to which they were subjected:

Negroes must know the history of the Negro race in
America, and this they will seldom get in white
institutions. Their children ought to study textbooks
like Brawley's "Short History," the first edition of
Woodson's "Negro in Our History," and Cromwell,
Turner, and Dykes' "Readings from Negro Authors."
Negroes who celebrate the birthdays of Washington
and Lincoln, and relatively unimportant "founders"
of various Negro colleges, ought not to forget the 5th
of March,—that first national holiday of this country,
which commemorates the martyrdom of Crispus At-
tucks. They ought to celebrate Negro Health Week
and Negro History Week. They ought to study
intelligently and from their own point of view, the
slave trade, slavery, emancipation, Reconstruction
and present economic development.[8]

Dr. DuBois proceeded then to explain in
careful detail that he was making no special
plea for segregated schools, or mixed schools,
but for *education*. To use his language:

---

[7] W. E. Burghardt DuBois "Does the Negro Need Separate
Schools?" *Journal of Negro Education* Volume IV No. 3, July,
1935. pp. 328-329

[8] *ibid.* p. 333

> . . . a separate Negro school where children are
> treated like human beings, trained by teachers of
> their own race, who know what it means to be black
> in the year of salvation 1935, is infinitely better than
> making our boys and girls doormats to be spit and
> trampled upon and lied to by ignorant social climb-
> ers, whose sole claim to superiority is ability to kick
> "niggers" when they are down.[9]

The foregoing observations relate directly to
the problems of *mis-education,* well understood
and posed by Woodson; and the same problems
are at long last being faced and attacked by the
very universities identified by DuBois and
many others. These institutions, formerly
known only as "white" colleges, are now heed-
ing the black demands, and are soliciting black
students, even at the expense of the "quota
systems," once so firmly entrenched. The "cry
in the wilderness" of Woodson in *Mis-
Education,* and his few like-minded cohorts,
has become a resounding chorus, and the rever-
berations will in time shake the *mis* from *Mis-
education.*

The scholars under discussion all shared a
common goal, namely, to provide for Negro
youth access to historical information and education which would be *true* and thus nullify or
diminish the false and belittling propaganda
type of history which had been handed to them
by whites. This, it was felt, would build up the

---

[9] *ibid.* p. 335

black child's self and race knowledge as well as his self-respect. In a larger sense they expected that their publications would at least partly fill the unjustifiable void in American History and its antecedents, reveal the existing distortions of actual facts, and constitute a service to the entire field of historical and social science writing and understanding.

Ultimately, thought Woodson and those who had similar beliefs, the program would be a responsible factor in regenerating race relations in all areas and not only in education. Without detracting from any other efforts (and there were others) it is reasonably certain that those writers who tried so zealously to right the wrongs of *mis-education* exerted a positive influence in that direction. As a result the democratic practices of this society are beginning to reach for its ideology, thus narrowing the long-existing cultural lag.

It is, in fact, quite clear that Woodson regarded this book as historical only in its most inclusive sense—history as interrelated with social customs, literature, economic and political matters and all else that affects society. This is a sensible and legitimate approach, as such historians as Spengler and Toynbee have demonstrated by popularizing broad areas and issues. Woodson was familiar with the tendency to include the intangible factors that influence the course of history—psychological elements and traditional sensitivities, based of course on valid historical methodology. He fitted *Mis-Education* into that framework.

Necessarily he thought in terms of other aspects of society which influenced education and which were, in turn influenced by it, because all of his writings show that he was convinced of the interrelations of all types of social phenomena. Furthermore, when he published *Mis-Education,* the nation was in the throes of a paralyzing economic depression, and President Franklin D. Roosevelt was on the verge of his vigorous and innovative administration. The "separate but equal" myth then afforded respectable legal sanction for an unequal, caste-like society, in education and all areas of national life. Permissive resignation had settled over much of the Negro population, and a majority rationalized that the caricature of education that they received was at least "better than it used to be."

The debilitating depression had thrust the problems of the Negro, as the lowest socio-economic class, into the forefront of those in dire need. As an educator of stature who was already engaged in his intensive writing and publishing program, the role of the disadvantageous educational system in keeping the black people on the lowest level, became abundantly clear to Woodson. Hence his attempts to analyze the problem and to define and castigate the type of education that confined Negroes in a vice-like grip of inferiority was designed not only to inform other historians and educators of their own derelictions, but to arouse the black people from their apathy. *Mis-Education* did not immediately have the impact that he hoped, but in the long run it merges now with the researches of the awakened historians and other educators; the demands of several minority groups, which have discovered each other; the insistence of students on racial equality and relevant curricula; and the clamor of the down-trodden masses for appropriate treatment as fellow human beings.

Dr. Woodson, in adopting a comprehensive, overall view of the problem of education in this book, was strongly prophetic, and showed a rare intellectual kinship with those who would move to the forefront in the next generation. His statement (p. 114), "The warring area, then, is in the cities," is highly pertinent to current circumstances, as are also the points in context which he connected with it. Another idea that he expressed with clarity (p. 117) in the sentences which follow, will be recognized at once for its present relevance:

> The race will free itself from exploiters just as soon as it decides to do so. No one else can accomplish this task for the race. It must plan and do for itself.

Another matter connected with *Mis-education* should be noted. The inferior character of black education was made inevitable by virtue of the poor financing of the segregated school systems. Although most Northern states had some racially-mixed schools, education in the sixteen southern, former slave states, plus Oklahoma and the District of Columbia, forming a bloc, provided the pattern, the atmosphere, and the reflection of Negro problems and general attitudes of whites about black education in the United States.

This southern bloc maintained a completely segregated system, and though there were differences in one category or another in spending money for education among its jurisdictions they had one common denominator—there were great differentials between moneys allocated for white education and black education. In 1930 the average expenditure per school-age child was $45.00 per white pupil and $14.95 per Negro pupil. Average southern investment in public school property per school-child amounted to $120.09 for whites and $29.62 for Negroes. Figures for 1928-1929 disclose that the average southern white teacher's pupil load was 31 for a school term of 164 days, while the average black teacher instructed about 44 pupils for 144 days. The average white teacher's salary was $1020, while the average black teacher earned $524.[10]

These figures were frustratingly well known to Dr. Woodson. As a participator in the field of education, an observer, a scholar and a reformer, he had long studied the disparties in the dual system. Before 1930 he had become thoroughly alarmed because the differentials between white and black education were increasing rather than diminishing, and that knowledge undoubtedly motivated some of the pessimism which creeps through in this volume.

Early in his Preface to *Mis-Education* the author takes a positive stand for tax money to be allocated in such manner that "every individual in the social order" should be given the opportunity to do his best. He rejected the objective notion of "progress" taken from statistical data, and injected a qualitative criteria which would judge the effectiveness of education by whether it was instrumental in making an individual "do and think for himself." With respect to Negro education in particular, it would require much study of the race and the role of its members in society. The dual system did not afford the opportunity for such study. As Woodson evaluated then, the inequity of the two societies within the nation, black and white, with its financial and propagandistic suppression of blacks through education and

---

[10] Monroe Work, *Negro Yearbook: An Annual Encyclopedia of the Negro 1931-1932.* Negro Yearbook Publishing Company. Tuskegee Institute Alabama, 1931. pp. 204, 205, 206.

otherwise, was efficiently responsible for the social ills that he so deplored. He was really aiming a direct blow at the rationale which the South used to justify the dual school system; and his position was vindicated by the United States 'Supreme Court in the 1950's, and subsequently by public opinion. When he suggested equal educational opportunities regardless of financial status or race he was more or less anticipating the ''social citizen'' concept of the incoming administration, although President Roosevelt did not implement his concept to its logical conclusion.

When Woodson likewise made observations to the effect that information alone was not education, he was not stating a unique or isolated theory. Other educators agreed, but many who professed to adhere to the notion did so in a merely abstract fashion. The author of this book very carefully elaborated and illustrated the thesis. He sought for meaningful, qualitative training, yet most educational institutions held fast to their rigid, inflexible programs, under which much of the required subject-matter might prove useful as intellectual discipline, but not to the life interests of the hapless, captive students. It was Woodson's idea that this system was most devastating to the black children whose schools were inferior, and whose future life interests were farthest removed from the traditional curricula. In recent years, and frequently by reason of student pressures, colleges have been reappraising and restructuring their programs, not necessarily because of Woodson's long-ago reasoning but surely in line with it.

The Preface to *Mis-Education* also contains a statement that the educational systems of both Europe and the United States were antiquated and failed to hit the mark for either race. A bold and daring assertion in 1933, to be sure, but Woodson had successfully pursued education in both Europe and America. It is evident now that his judgement was projected far beyond its utterance, as witness the student movements which are presently accelerating, and assuming differing and ever more demanding forms. In further attestation note also the trend toward "vocational" education; and the frenzied effort to incorporate Black Studies at all educational levels.

Indeed long before this present climactic phase, there had been a rising racial consciousness and a new stridency to the demands by American Negroes. By the start of World War II the sacred cow of segregation was being reexamined more vigorously than ever before. Such scholars as Frazier, Myrdal, Silberman and others were writing sociologically with candor and verve on racial problems, while Woodson continued his even and uninterrupted interpretation of these problems, plus writing historical books, papers, and engaging in other journalistic endeavors. Cynicism and disillusionment among blacks had spread and become crystallized into a determination to make equality real. The indictments against discrimination were even more virile than Woodson's had been in *Mis-Education* some years earlier, and they covered more thoroughly the entire spectrum of race relations, but there was a direct line of descent from the educational castigation of 1933 to the more vigorous racial agitation and writings of the next decade.

Carter G. Woodson did not propose, in *Mis-Education,* such drastic action as the mass protest movement of A. Phillip Randolph in 1941, but then he did not have the type of support which later materialized; nor had there been in 1933 the mass militancy to which World War II gave birth. His was a modest demand, as really were the goals of Randolph's movement when judged by the scope of later demands and achievements. But if one seeks to comprehend the present culmination period in race relations, he must turn back to those earlier efforts and acknowledge the ideas and the work which "seeded the ground" as it were, and made possible a climate of opinion within which concerted action for equality could germinate and grow to fruition. This intellectual climate was possible because the research, writings, and publications of a dedicated scholar like Woodson had provided the historical information, the impetus, and the inspiration for black people to acquire a worthwhile self and race image, to make a start toward overcoming the inferiority complex which had for so long been an emotional prison. Looking back in such manner is a major purpose of history, and in that context the reissuing of this book is both appropriate and necessary.

It will be of great interest for readers to note the similarity in Woodson, the critic, as he looks at education in his day and the day in which we live. Black youth seems to be asking for what Woodson wanted as he expressed it in these pages. His philosophy was not only sound for him but it is sound for them, as they make the same demands of administrators for Black Studies, Black Curricula and Black personnel. It is for this reason that we publish this volume. It had a message for Yesterday and it has a message which Black and white should know for Today.

CHARLES H. WESLEY AND THELMA D. PERRY

FOREWORD

The thoughts brought together in this volume have been expressed in recent addresses and articles written by the author. From time to time persons deeply interested in the point of view therein presented have requested that these comments on education be made available in book form. To supply this demand this volume is given to the public.

In the preparation of the volume the author has not followed in detail the productions upon which most of the book is based. The aim is to set forth only the thought developed in passing from the one to the other. The language in some cases, then, is entirely new; and the work is not a collection of essays. In this way repetition has been avoided except to emphasize the thesis which the author sustains.

CARTER GODWIN WOODSON

Washington, D. C.
January, 1933.

CONTENTS

CONTENTS

PREFACE

HEREIN are recorded not opinions but the reflections of one who for forty years has participated in the education of the black, brown, yellow and white races in both hemispheres and in tropical and temperate regions. Such experience, too, has been with students in all grades from the kindergarten to the university. The author, moreover, has traveled around the world to observe not only modern school systems in various countries but to study the special systems set up by private agencies and governments to educate the natives in their colonies and dependencies. Some of these observations, too, have been checked against more recent studies on a later tour.

Discussing herein the mistakes made in the education of the Negro, the writer frankly admits that he has committed some of these errors himself. In several chapters, moreover, he specifically points out wherein he himself has strayed from the path of wisdom. This book, then, is not intended as a broadside against any particular person or class, but it is given as a corrective for methods which have not produced satisfactory results.

The author does not support the once popular view that in matters of education Negroes are rightfully subjected to the will of others on the presumption that these poor people are not large taxpayers and must be content with charitable contributions to their uplift. The author takes the position that the consumer pays the tax, and as such every individual of the social order should be given unlimited opportunity to make the most of himself. Such opportunity, too, should not be determined from without by forces set to direct the proscribed element in a way to redound solely to the good of others but should be determined by the make-up of the Negro himself and by what his environment requires of him.

This new program of uplift, the author contends, should not be decided upon by the trial and error method in the application of devices used in dealing with others in a different situation and at another epoch. Only by careful study of the Negro himself and the life which he is forced to lead can we arrive at the proper procedure in this crisis. The mere imparting of information is not education. Above all things, the effort must result in making a man think and do for himself just as the Jews have done in spite of universal persecution.

In thus estimating the results obtained from the so-called education of the Negro the author does not go to the census figures to show the progress of the race. It may be of no importance to the race to be able to boast today of many times as many "educated" members as it had in 1865. If they are of the wrong kind the increase in numbers will be a disadvantage rather than an advantage. The only question which concerns us here is whether these "educated" persons are actually equipped to face the ordeal before them or unconsciously contribute to their own undoing by perpetuating the regime of the oppressor.

Herein, however, lies no argument for the oft-heard contention that education for the white man should mean one thing and for the Negro a different thing. The element of race does not enter here. It is merely a matter of exercising common sense in approaching people through their environment in order to deal with conditions as they are rather than as you would like to see them or imagine that they are. There may be a difference in method of attack, but the principle remains the same.

"Highly educated" Negroes denounce persons who advocate for the Negro a sort of education different in some respects from that now given the white man. Negroes who have been so long inconvenienced and denied opportunities for development are naturally afraid of anything that sounds like discrimination. They are anxious to have everything the white man has even if it is harmful. The possibility of originality in the Negro, therefore, is discounted one hundred per cent to maintain a nominal equality. If the whites decide to take up Mormonism the Negroes must follow their lead. If the whites neglect such a study, then the Negroes must do likewise.

The author, however, does not have such an attitude. He considers the educational system as it has developed both in Europe and America an antiquated process which does not hit the mark even in the case of the needs of the white man himself. If the white man wants to hold on to it, let him do so; but the Negro, so far as he is able, should develop and carry out a program of his own.

The so-called modern education, with all its defects, however, does others so much more good than it does the Negro, because it has been worked out in conformity to the needs of those who have enslaved and oppressed weaker peoples. For example, the philosophy and ethics resulting from our educational system have justified slavery, peonage, segregation, and lynching. The oppressor has the right to exploit, to handicap, and to kill the oppressed. Negroes daily educated in the tenets of such a religion of the strong have accepted the status of the weak as divinely ordained, and during the last three generations of their nominal freedom they have done practically nothing to change it. Their pouting and resolutions indulged in by a few of the race have been of little avail.

No systematic effort toward change has been possible, for, taught the same economics, history, philosophy, literature and religion which have established the present code of morals, the Negro's mind has been brought under the control of his oppressor. The problem of holding the Negro down, therefore, is easily solved. When you control a man's thinking you do not have to worry about his actions. You do not have to tell him not to stand here or go yonder. He will find his "proper place" and will stay in it. You do not need to send him to the back door. He will go without being told. In fact, if there is no back door, he will cut one for his special benefit. His education makes it necessary.

The same educational process which inspires and stimulates the oppressor with the thought that he is everything and has accomplished everything worth while, depresses and crushes at the same time the spark of genius in the Negro by making him feel that his race does not amount to much and never will measure up to the standards of other peoples. The Negro thus educated is a hopeless liability of the race.

The difficulty is that the "educated Negro" is compelled to live and move among his own people whom he has been taught to despise. As a rule, therefore, the "educated Negro" prefers to buy his food from a white grocer because he has been taught that the Negro is not clean. It does not matter how often a Negro washes his hands, then, he cannot clean them, and it does not matter how often a white man uses his hands he cannot soil them. The educated Negro, moreover, is disinclined to take part in Negro business, because he has been taught in economics that Negroes cannot operate in this particular sphere. The "educated Negro" gets less and less pleasure out of the Negro church, not on account of its primitiveness and increasing corruption, but because of his preference for the seats of "righteousness" controlled by his oppressor. This has been his education, and nothing else can be expected of him.

If the "educated Negro" could go off and be white he might be happy, but only a mulatto now and then can do this. The large majority of this class, then, must go through life denouncing white people because they are trying to run away from the blacks and decrying the blacks because they are not white.

THE MIS-EDUCATION
OF THE NEGRO

THE MIS-EDUCATION
OF THE NEGRO

CHAPTER I

THE SEAT OF THE TROUBLE

THE "educated Negroes" have the attitude of contempt toward their own people because in their own as well as in their mixed schools Negroes are taught to admire the Hebrew, the Greek, the Latin and the Teuton and to despise the African. Of the hundreds of Negro high schools recently examined by an expert in the United States Bureau of Education only eighteen offer a course taking up the history of the Negro, and in most of the Negro colleges and universities where the Negro is thought of, the race is studied only as a problem or dismissed as of little consequence. For example, an officer of a Negro university, thinking that an additional course on the Negro should be given there, called upon a Negro Doctor of Philosophy of the faculty to offer such work. He promptly informed the officer that he knew nothing about the Negro. He did not go to school to waste his time that way. He went to be educated in a system which dismisses the Negro as a nonentity.

At a Negro summer school two years ago, a white instructor gave a course on the Negro, using for his text a work which teaches that whites are superior to the blacks. When asked by one of the students why he used such a textbook the instructor replied that he wanted them to get that point of view. Even schools for Negroes, then, are places where they must be convinced of their inferiority.

The thought of the inferiority of the Negro is drilled into him in almost every class he enters and in almost every book he studies. If he happens to leave school after he masters the fundamentals, before he finishes high school or reaches college, he will naturally escape some of this bias and may recover in time to be of service to his people.

Practically all of the successful Negroes in this country are of the uneducated type or of that of Negroes who have had no formal education at all. The large majority of the Negroes who have put on the finishing touches of our best colleges are all but worthless in the development of their people. If after leaving school they have the opportunity to give out to Negroes what traducers of the race would like to have it learn such persons may thereby earn a living at teaching or preaching what they have been taught but they never become a con-

2

structive force in the development of the race. The so-called school, then, becomes a questionable factor in the life of this despised people.

As another has well said, to handicap a student by teaching him that his black face is a curse and that his struggle to change his condition is hopeless is the worst sort of lynching. It kills one's aspirations and dooms him to vagabondage and crime. It is strange, then, that the friends of truth and the promoters of freedom have not risen up against the present propaganda in the schools and crushed it. This crusade is much more important than the anti-lynching movement, because there would be no lynching if it did not start in the schoolroom. Why not exploit, enslave, or exterminate a class that everybody is taught to regard as inferior?

To be more explicit we may go to the seat of the trouble. Our most widely known scholars have been trained in universities outside of the South. Northern and Western institutions, however, have had no time to deal with matters which concern the Negro especially. They must direct their attention to the problems of the majority of their constituents, and too often they have stimulated their prejudices by referring to the Negro as unworthy of consideration. Most of what these universities have offered as language, mathematics, and science may have served a good purpose, but much of what they have taught as economics, history, literature, religion and philosophy is propaganda and cant that involved a waste of time and misdirected the Negroes thus trained.

And even in the certitude of science or mathematics it has been unfortunate that the approach to the Negro has been borrowed from a "foreign" method. For example, the teaching of arithmetic in the fifth grade in a backward county in Mississippi should mean one thing in the Negro school and a decidedly different thing in the white school. The Negro children, as a rule, come from the homes of tenants and peons who have to migrate annually from plantation to plantation, looking for light which they have never seen. The children from the homes of white planters and merchants live permanently in the midst of calculations, family budgets, and the like, which enable them sometimes to learn more by contact than the Negro can acquire in school. Instead of teaching such Negro children less arithmetic, they should be taught much more of it than the white children, for the latter attend a graded school consolidated by free transportation when the Negroes go to one-room rented hovels to be taught without equipment and by incompetent teachers educated scarcely beyond the eighth grade.

In schools of theology Negroes are taught the interpretation of the Bible worked out by those who have justified segregation and winked at the economic debasement of the Negro sometimes almost to the point of starvation. Deriving their sense of right from this teaching, graduates of such schools can have no message to grip the people whom they have been ill trained to serve. Most of such mis-educated ministers, therefore, preach to benches while illiterate Negro preachers do the best they can in supplying the spiritual needs of the masses.

In the schools of business administration Negroes are trained exclusively in the psychology and economics of Wall Street and are, therefore, made to despise the opportunities to run ice wagons, push banana carts, and sell peanuts among their own people. Foreigners, who have not studied economics but have studied Negroes, take up this business and grow rich.

In schools of journalism Negroes are being taught how to edit such metropolitan dailies as the *Chicago Tribune* and the *New York Times,* which would hardly hire a Negro as a janitor; and when these graduates come to the Negro weeklies for employment they are not prepared to function in such establishments, which, to be successful, must be built upon accurate knowledge of the psychology and philosophy of the Negro.

When a Negro has finished his education in our schools, then, he has been equipped to begin the life of an Americanized or Europeanized white man, but before he steps from the threshold of his alma mater he is told by his teachers that he must go back to his own people from whom he has been estranged by a vision of ideals which in his disillusionment he will realize that he cannot attain. He goes forth to play his part in life, but he must be both social and bisocial at the same time. While he is a part of the body politic, he is in addition to this a member of a particular race to which he must restrict himself in all matters social. While serving his country he must serve within a special group. While being a good American, he must above all things be a "good Negro"; and to perform this definite function he must learn to stay in a "Negro's place."

For the arduous task of serving a race thus handicapped, however, the Negro graduate has had little or no training at all. The people whom he has been ordered to serve have been belittled by his teachers to the extent that he can hardly find delight in undertaking what his education has led him to think is impossible. Considering his race as blank in achievement, then, he sets out to stimulate their imitation of others. The performance is kept up a while; but, like any other effort at meaningless imitation, it results in failure.

Facing this undesirable result, the highly educated Negro often grows sour. He becomes too pessimistic to be a constructive force and usually develops into a chronic fault-finder or a complainant at the bar of public opinion. Often when he sees that the fault lies at the door of the white oppressor whom he is afraid to attack, he turns upon the pioneering Negro who is at work doing the best he can to extricate himself from an uncomfortable predicament.

In this effort to imitate, however, these "educated people" are sincere. They hope to make the Negro conform quickly to the standard of the whites and thus remove the pretext for the barriers between the races. They do not realize, however, that even if the Negroes do successfully imitate the whites, nothing new has thereby been accomplished. You simply have a larger number of persons doing what others have been doing. The unusual gifts of the race have not thereby been developed, and an unwilling world, therefore, continues to wonder what the Negro is good for.

These "educated" people, however, decry any such thing as race consciousness; and in some respects they are right. They do not like to hear such expressions as "Negro literature," "Negro poetry," "African art," or "thinking black"; and, roughly speaking, we must concede that such things do not exist. These things did not figure in the courses which they pursued in school, and why should they? "Aren't we all Americans? Then, whatever is American is as much the heritage of the Negro as of any other group in this country."

The "highly educated" contend, moreover,

that when the Negro emphasizes these things he invites racial discrimination by recognizing such differentness of the races. The thought that the Negro is one thing and the white man another is the stock-in-trade argument of the Caucasian to justify segregation. Why, then, should the Negro blame the white man for doing what he himself does?

These "highly educated" Negroes, however, fail to see that it is not the Negro who takes this position. The white man forces him to it, and to extricate himself therefrom the Negro leader must so deal with the situation as to develop in the segregated group the power with which they can elevate themselves. The differentness of races, moreover, is no evidence of superiority or of inferiority. This merely indicates that each race has certain gifts which the others do not possess. It is by the development of these gifts that every race must justify its right to exist.

CHAPTER II

HOW WE MISSED THE MARK

How we have arrived at the present state of affairs can be understood only by studying the forces effective in the development of Negro education since it was systematically undertaken immediately after Emancipation. To point out merely the defects as they appear today will be of little benefit to the present and future generations. These things must be viewed in their historic setting. The conditions of today have been determined by what has taken place in the past, and in a careful study of this history we may see more clearly the great theatre of events in which the Negro has played a part. We may understand better what his rôle has been and how well he has functioned in it.

The idea of educating the Negroes after the Civil War was largely a prompting of philanthropy. Their white neighbors failed to assume this responsibility. These black people had been liberated as a result of a sectional conflict out of which their former owners had emerged as victims. From this class, then, the freedmen could not expect much sympathy or cooperation in the effort to prepare themselves to figure as citizens of a modern republic.

From functionaries of the United States Government itself and from those who participated in the conquest of the secessionists early came the plan of teaching these freedmen the simple duties of life as worked out by the Freedmen's Bureau and philanthropic agencies. When systematized this effort became a program for the organization of churches and schools and the direction of them along lines which had been considered most conducive to the progress of people otherwise circumstanced. Here and there some variation was made in this program in view of the fact that the status of the freedmen in no way paralleled that of their friends and teachers, but such thought was not general. When the Negroes in some way would learn to perform the duties which other elements of the population had prepared themselves to discharge they would be duly qualified, it was believed, to function as citizens of the country.

Inasmuch as most Negroes lived in the agricultural South, moreover, and only a few of them at first acquired small farms there was little in their life which any one of thought could not have easily understood. The poverty which afflicted them for a generation after Emancipation held them down to the lowest order of society, nominally free but economically enslaved. The participation of the freedmen in government for a few years during the period known as the Reconstruction had little bearing on their situation except that they did join with the uneducated poor whites in bringing about certain much-desired social reforms, especially in giving the South its first plan of democratic education in providing for a school system at public expense.

Neither this inadequately supported school system nor the struggling higher institutions of a classical order established about the same time, however, connected the Negroes very closely with life as it was. These institutions were concerned rather with life as they hoped to make it. When the Negro found himself deprived of influence in politics, therefore, and at the same time unprepared to participate in the higher functions in the industrial development which this country began to undergo, it soon became evident to him that he was losing ground in the basic things of life. He was spending his time studying about the things which had been or might be, but he was learning little to help him to do better the tasks at hand. Since the Negroes believed that the causes of this untoward condition lay without the race, migration was attempted, and emigration to Africa was again urged. At this psychological moment came the wave of industrial education which swept the country by storm. The educational authorities in the cities and States throughout the Black Belt began to change the course of study to make the training of the Negro conform to this policy.

The missionary teachers from the North in defense of their idea of more liberal training, however, fearlessly attacked this new educational policy; and the Negroes participating in the same dispute arrayed themselves respectively on one side or the other. For a generation thereafter the quarrel as to whether the Negro should be given a classical or a practical education was the dominant topic in Negro schools and churches throughout the United States. Labor was the most important thing of life, it was argued; practical education counted in reaching that end; and the Negro worker must be taught to solve this problem of efficiency before directing attention to other things.

Others more narrow-minded than the advocates of industrial education, seized upon the idea, feeling that, although the Negro must have some semblance of education, it would be a fine stroke to be able to make a distinction between the training given the Negro and that provided for the whites. Inasmuch as the industrial educational idea rapidly gained ground, too, many Negroes for political purposes began to espouse it; and schools and colleges hoping thereby to obtain money worked out accordingly makeshift provisions for such instruction, although they could not satisfactorily offer it. A few real industrial schools actually equipped themselves for this work and turned out a number of graduates with such preparation.

Unfortunately, however, the affair developed into a sort of battle of words, for in spite of all they said and did the majority of the Negroes, those who did make some effort to obtain an education, did not actually receive either the industrial or the classical education. Negroes attended industrial schools, took such training as was prescribed, and received their diplomas; but few of them developed adequate efficiency to be able to do what they were supposedly trained to do. The schools in which they were educated could not provide for all the experience with machinery which white apprentices trained in factories had. Such industrial education as these Negroes received, then, was merely to master a technique already discarded in progressive centres; and even in less complicated operations of industry these schools had no such facilities as to parallel the numerous processes of factories conducted on the plan of the division of labor. Except what value such training might have in the development of the mind by making practical applications of mathematics and science, then, it was a failure.

The majority of Negro graduates of industrial schools, therefore, have gone into other avenues, and too often into those for which they have had no preparation whatever. Some few who actually prepared for the industrial sphere by self-improvement likewise sought other occupations for the reason that Negroes were generally barred from higher pursuits by trades unions; and, being unable to develop captains of industry to increase the demand for persons in these lines, the Negroes have not opened up many such opportunities for themselves.

During these years, too, the schools for the classical education for Negroes have not done any better. They have proceeded on the basis that every ambitious person needs a liberal education when as a matter of fact this does not necessarily follow. The Negro trained in the advanced phases of literature, philosophy, and politics has been unable to develop far in using his knowledge because of having to function in the lower spheres of the social order. Advanced knowledge of science, mathematics and languages, moreover, has not been much more useful except for mental discipline because of the dearth of opportunity to apply such knowledge among people who were largely common laborers in towns or peons on the plantations. The extent to which such higher education has been successful in leading the Negro to think, which above all is the chief purpose of education, has merely made him more of a malcontent when he can sense the drift of things and appreciate the impossibility of success in visioning conditions as they really are.

It is very clear, therefore, that we do not have in the life of the Negro today a large number of persons who have been benefited by either of the systems about which we have quarreled so long. The number of Negro mechanics and artisans have comparatively declined during the last two generations. The Negroes do not proportionately represent as many skilled laborers as they did before the Civil War. If the practical education which the Negroes received helped to improve the situation so that it is today no worse than what it is, certainly it did not solve the problem as was expected of it.

On the other hand, in spite of much classical education of the Negroes we do not find in the race a large supply of thinkers and philosophers. One excuse is that scholarship among Negroes has been vitiated by the necessity for all of them to combat segregation and fight to retain standing ground in the struggle of the races. Comparatively few American Negroes have produced creditable literature, and still fewer have made any large contribution to philosophy or science. They have not risen to the heights of black men farther removed from the influences of slavery and segregation. For this reason we do not find among American Negroes a Pushkin, a Gomez, a Geoffrey, a Captein or a Dumas. Even men like Roland Hayes and Henry O. Tanner have risen to the higher levels by getting out of this country to relieve themselves of our stifling traditions and to recover from their education.

CHAPTER III

How, then, did the education of the Negro take such a trend? The people who maintained schools for the education of certain Negroes before the Civil War were certainly sincere; and so were the missionary workers who went South to enlighten the freedmen after the results of that conflict had given the Negroes a new status. These earnest workers, however, had more enthusiasm than knowledge. They did not understand the task before them. This undertaking, too, was more of an effort toward social uplift than actual education. Their aim was to transform the Negroes, not to develop them. The freedmen who were to be enlightened were given little thought, for the best friends of the race, ill-taught themselves, followed the traditional curricula of the times which did not take the Negro into consideration except to condemn or pity him.

In geography the races were described in conformity with the program of the usual propaganda to engender in whites a race hate of the Negro, and in the Negroes contempt for themselves. A poet of distinction was selected to

17

illustrate the physical features of the white race, a bedecked chief of a tribe those of the red, a proud warrior the brown, a prince the yellow, and a savage with a ring in his nose the black. The Negro, of course, stood at the foot of the social ladder.

The description of the various parts of the world was worked out according to the same plan. The parts inhabited by the Caucasian were treated in detail. Less attention was given to the yellow people, still less to the red, very little to the brown, and practically none to the black race. Those people who are far removed from the physical characteristics of the Caucasians or who do not materially assist them in the domination or exploitation of others were not mentioned except to be belittled or decried.

From the teaching of science the Negro was likewise eliminated. The beginnings of science in various parts of the Orient were mentioned, but the Africans' early advancement in this field was omitted. Students were not told that ancient Africans of the interior knew sufficient science to concoct poisons for arrowheads, to mix durable colors for paintings, to extract metals from nature and refine them for development in the industrial arts. Very little was said about the chemistry in the method of Egyptian embalming which was the product of the mixed breeds of Northern Africa, now known in the modern world as "colored people."

In the study of language in school pupils were made to scoff at the Negro dialect as some peculiar possession of the Negro which they should despise rather than directed to study the background of this language as a broken-down African tongue—in short to understand their own linguistic history, which is certainly more important for them than the study of French Phonetics or Historical Spanish Grammar. To the African language as such no attention was given except in case of the preparation of traders, missionaries and public functionaries to exploit the natives. This number of persons thus trained, of course, constituted a small fraction hardly deserving attention.

From literature the African was excluded altogether. He was not supposed to have expressed any thought worth knowing. The philosophy in the African proverbs and in the rich folklore of that continent was ignored to give preference to that developed on the distant shores of the Mediterranean. Most missionary teachers of the freedmen, like most men of our time, had never read the interesting books of travel in Africa, and had never heard of the *Tarikh Es-Soudan.*

In the teaching of fine arts these instructors usually started with Greece by showing how that art was influenced from without, but they omitted the African influence which scientists now regard as significant and dominant in early Hellas. They failed to teach the student the Mediterranean Melting Pot with the Negroes from Africa bringing their wares, their ideas and their blood therein to influence the history of Greece, Carthage, and Rome. Making desire father to the thought, our teachers either ignored these influences or endeavored to belittle them by working out theories to the contrary.

The bias did not stop at this point, for it invaded the teaching of the professions. Negro law students were told that they belonged to the most criminal element in the country; and an effort was made to justify the procedure in the seats of injustice where law was interpreted as being one thing for the white man and a different thing for the Negro. In constitutional law the spinelessness of the United States Supreme Court in permitting the judicial nullification of the Fourteenth and Fifteenth Amendments was and still is boldly upheld in our few law schools.

In medical schools Negroes were likewise convinced of their inferiority in being reminded of their rôle as germ carriers. The prevalence of syphilis and tuberculosis among Negroes was especially emphasized without showing that these maladies are more deadly among the Negroes for the reason that they are Caucasian diseases; and since these plagues are new to

Negroes, these sufferers have not had time to develop against them the immunity which time has permitted in the Caucasian. Other diseases to which Negroes easily fall prey were mentioned to point out the race as an undesirable element when this condition was due to the Negroes' economic and social status. Little emphasis was placed upon the immunity of the Negro from diseases like yellow fever and influenza which are so disastrous to whites. Yet, the whites were not considered inferior because of this differential resistance to these plagues.

In history, of course, the Negro had no place in this curriculum. He was pictured as a human being of the lower order, unable to subject passion to reason, and therefore useful only when made the hewer of wood and the drawer of water for others. No thought was given to the history of Africa except so far as it had been a field of exploitation for the Caucasian. You might study the history as it was offered in our system from the elementary school throughout the university, and you would never hear Africa mentioned except in the negative. You would never thereby learn that Africans first domesticated the sheep, goat, and cow, developed the idea of trial by jury, produced the first stringed instruments, and gave the world its greatest boon in the discovery of iron. You would never know that prior to the Mohammedan invasion about 1000 A.D. these natives in the heart of Africa had developed powerful kingdoms which were later organized as the Songhay Empire on the order of that of the Romans and boasting of similar grandeur.

Unlike other people, then, the Negro, according to this point of view, was an exception to the natural plan of things, and he had no such mission as that of an outstanding contribution to culture. The status of the Negro, then, was justly fixed as that of an inferior. Teachers of Negroes in their first schools after Emancipation did not proclaim any such doctrine, but the content of their curricula justified these inferences.

An observer from outside of the situation naturally inquires why the Negroes, many of whom serve their race as teachers, have not changed this program. These teachers, however, are powerless. Negroes have no control over their education and have little voice in their other affairs pertaining thereto. In a few cases Negroes have been chosen as members of public boards of education, and some have been appointed members of private boards, but these Negroes are always such a small minority that they do not figure in the final working out of the educational program. The education of the Negroes, then, the most important thing in the uplift of the Negroes, is almost entirely in the hands of those who have enslaved them and now segregate them.

With "mis-educated Negroes" in control themselves, however, it is doubtful that the system would be very much different from what it is or that it would rapidly undergo change. The Negroes thus placed in charge would be the products of the same system and would show no more conception of the task at hand than do the whites who have educated them and shaped their minds as they would have them function. Negro educators of today may have more sympathy and interest in the race than the whites now exploiting Negro institutions as educators, but the former have no more vision than their competitors. Taught from books of the same bias, trained by Caucasians of the same prejudices or by Negroes of enslaved minds, one generation of Negro teachers after another have served for no higher purpose than to do what they are told to do. In other words, a Negro teacher instructing Negro children is in many respects a white teacher thus engaged, for the program in each case is about the same.

There can be no reasonable objection to the Negro's doing what the white man tells him to do, if the white man tells him to do what is right; but right is purely relative. The present system under the control of the whites trains the Negro to be white and at the same time convinces him of the impropriety or the impossibility of his becoming white. It compels the Negro to become a good Negro for the performance of which his education is ill-suited. For the white man's exploitation of the Negro through economic restriction and segregation the present system is sound and will doubtless continue until this gives place to the saner policy of actual interracial cooperation—not the present farce of racial manipulation in which the Negro is a figurehead. History does not furnish a case of the elevation of a people by ignoring the thought and aspiration of the people thus served.

This is slightly dangerous ground here, however, for the Negro's mind has been all but perfectly enslaved in that he has been trained to think what is desired of him. The "highly educated" Negroes do not like to hear anything uttered against this procedure because they make their living in this way, and they feel that they must defend the system. Few mis-educated Negroes ever act otherwise; and, if they so express themselves, they are easily crushed by the large majority to the contrary so that the procession may move on without interruption.

The result, then, is that the Negroes thus mis-educated are of no service to themselves and none to the white man. The white man does not need the Negroes' professional, commercial or industrial assistance; and as a result of the multiplication of mechanical appliances he no longer needs them in drudgery or menial service. The "highly educated" Negroes, moreover, do not need the Negro professional or commercial classes because Negroes have been taught that whites can serve them more efficiently in these spheres. Reduced, then, to teaching and preaching, the Negroes will have no outlet but to go down a blind alley, if the sort of education which they are now receiving is to enable them to find the way out of their present difficulties.

CHAPTER IV

EDUCATION UNDER OUTSIDE CONTROL

"In the new program of educating the Negro what would become of the white teachers of the race?" some one recently inquired. This is a simple question requiring only a brief answer. The remaining few Christian workers who went South not so long after the Civil War and established schools and churches to lay the foundation on which we should now be building more wisely than we do, we would honor as a martyred throng. Anathema be upon him who would utter a word derogatory to the record of these heroes and heroines! We would pay high tribute also to unselfish Southerners like Haygood, Curry, Ruffner, Northern, and Vance, and to white men of our time, who believe that the only way to elevate people is to help them to help themselves.

The unfortunate successors of the Northern missionary teachers of Negroes, however, have thoroughly demonstrated that they have no useful function in the life of the Negro. They have not the spirit of their predecessors and do not measure up to the requirements of educators desired in accredited colleges. If Negro institutions are to be as efficient as those for the whites in the South the same high standard for the educators to direct them should be maintained. Negro schools cannot go forward with such a load of inefficiency and especially when the white presidents of these institutions are often less scholarly than Negroes who have to serve under them.

By law and custom the white presidents and teachers of Negro schools are prevented from participating freely in the life of the Negro. They occupy, therefore, a most uncomfortable dual position. When the author once taught in a school with a mixed faculty the white women connected with the institution would bow to him in patronizing fashion when on the campus, but elsewhere they did not see him. A white president of one Negro school never entertains a Negro in his home, preferring to shift such guests to the students' dining-room. Another white president of a Negro college maintains on the campus a guest cottage which Negroes can enter only as servants. Still another such functionary does not allow students to enter his home through the front door. Negroes trained under such conditions without protest become downright cowards, and in life will continue as slaves in spite of their nominal emancipation.

"What different method of approach or what sort of appeal would one make to the Negro child that cannot be made just as well by a

white teacher?'' some one asked not long ago.
To be frank we must concede that there is no
particular body of facts that Negro teachers
can impart to children of their own race that
may not be just as easily presented by persons
of another race if they have the same attitude
as Negro teachers; but in most cases tradition,
race hate, segregation, and terrorism make such
a thing impossible. The only thing to do in this
case, then, is to deal with the situation as it is.

Yet we should not take the position that a
qualified white person should not teach in a
Negro school. For certain work which temporarily some whites may be able to do better than
the Negroes there can be no objection to such
service, but if the Negro is to be forced to live in
the ghetto he can more easily develop out of it
under his own leadership than under that which
is super-imposed. The Negro will never be able
to show all of his originality as long as his efforts are directed from without by those who
socially proscribe him. Such ''friends'' will
unconsciously keep him in the ghetto.

Herein, however, the emphasis is not upon
the necessity for separate systems but upon the
need for common sense schools and teachers
who understand and continue in sympathy with
those whom they instruct. Those who take the
position to the contrary have the idea that education is merely a process of imparting information. One who can give out these things or

devise an easy plan for so doing, then, is an educator. In a sense this is true, but it accounts for most of the troubles of the Negro. Real education means to inspire people to live more abundantly, to learn to begin with life as they find it and make it better, but the instruction so far given Negroes in colleges and universities has worked to the contrary. In most cases such graduates have merely increased the number of malcontents who offer no program for changing the undesirable conditions about which they complain. One should rely upon protest only when it is supported by a constructive program.

Unfortunately Negroes who think as the author does and dare express themselves are branded as opponents of interracial cooperation. As a matter of fact, however, such Negroes are the real workers in carrying out a program of interracial effort. Cooperation implies equality of the participants in the particular task at hand. On the contrary, however, the usual way now is for the whites to work out their plans behind closed doors, have them approved by a few Negroes serving nominally on a board, and then employ a white or mixed staff to carry out their program. This is not interracial cooperation. It is merely the ancient idea of calling upon the "inferior" to carry out the orders of the "superior." To express it in post-classic language, as did Jessie O. Thomas, "The Negroes do the 'coing' and the whites the 'operating.'"

This unsound attitude of the "friends" of the Negro is due to the persistence of the mediaeval idea of controlling underprivileged classes. Behind closed doors these "friends" say you need to be careful in advancing Negroes to commanding positions unless it can be determined beforehand that they will do what they are told to do. You can never tell when some Negroes will break out and embarrass their "friends." After being advanced to positions of influence some of them have been known to run amuck and advocate social equality or demand for their race the privileges of democracy when they should restrict themselves to education and religious development.

It is often said, too, that the time is not ripe for Negroes to take over the administration of their institutions, for they do not have the contacts for raising money; but what becomes of this argument when we remember what Booker T. Washington did for Tuskegee and observe what R. R. Moton and John Hope are doing today? As the first Negro president of Howard University Mordecai W. Johnson has raised more money for that institution among philanthropists than all of its former presidents combined. Furthermore, if, after three generations the Negro colleges have not produced men qualified to administer their affairs, such an admission is an eloquent argument that they have failed ingloriously and should be immediately closed.

Recently some one asked me how I connect my criticism of the higher education of the Negroes with new developments in this sphere and especially with the four universities in the South which are to be made possible by the millions obtained from governments, boards, and philanthropists. I believe that the establishment of these four centres of learning at Washington, Atlanta, Nashville, and New Orleans can be so carried out as to mark an epoch in the development of the Negro race. On the other hand, there is just as much possibility for a colossal failure of the whole scheme. If these institutions are to be the replica of universities like Harvard, Yale, Columbia and Chicago, if the men who are to administer them and teach in them are to be the products of roll-top desk theorists who have never touched the life of the Negro, the money thus invested will be just as profitably spent if it is used to buy peanuts to throw at the animals in a circus.

Some of the thought behind the new educational movement is to provide in the South for educating the Negroes who are now crowding Northern universities, especially the medical schools, many of which will not admit Negroes because of the racial friction in hospital practice. In the rush merely to make special provisions for these "undesirable students," however, the institutions which are to train them may be established on false ideas and make the same blunders of the smaller institutions which have preceded them. It will hardly help a poisoned patient to give him a large dose of poison.

In higher institutions for Negroes, organized along lines required for people differently circumstanced, some few may profit by being further grounded in the fundamentals, others may become more adept in the exploitation of their people, and a smaller number may cross the divide and join the whites in useful service; but the large majority of the products of such institutions will increase rather than diminish the load which the masses have had to carry ever since their emancipation. Such ill-prepared workers will have no foundation upon which to build. The education of any people should begin with the people themselves, but Negroes thus trained have been dreaming about the ancients of Europe and about those who have tried to imitate them.

In a course at Harvard, for example, students were required to find out whether Pericles was justly charged with trying to supplant the worship of Jupiter with that of Juno. Since that time Negroes thus engaged have learned that they would have been much better prepared for work among the Negroes in the Black Belt if they had spent that time learning why John

Jasper of "sun-do-move" fame joined with Joshua in contending that the planet stood still "in the middle of the line while he fought the battle the second time."

Talking the other day with one of the men now giving the millions to build the four Negro universities in the South, however, I find that he is of the opinion that accredited institutions can be established in mushroom fashion with theorists out of touch with the people. In other words, you can go almost anywhere and build a three million dollar plant, place in charge a white man to do what you want accomplished, and in a short while he can secure or have trained to order the men necessary to make a university. "We want here," he will say, "a man who has his Master's degree in English. Send me another who has his Doctor's degree in sociology, and I can use one more in physics."

Now, experience has shown that men of this type may "fill in," but a university cannot be established with such raw recruits. The author once had some experience in trying to man a college in this fashion, and the result was a story that would make an interesting headline for the newspapers. When Dr. William Rainey Harper was establishing the University of Chicago he called to the headship of the various departments only men who had distinguished themselves in the creative world. Some had advanced degrees, and some had not. Several of them had never done any formal graduate work at all. All of them, however, were men whose thought was moving the world. It may be argued that the Negroes have no such men and must have them trained, but such a thing cannot be forced as we are now doing it. It would be much better to stimulate the development of the more progressive teachers of old than experiment with novices produced by the degradation of higher education.

The degradation of the doctorate especially dawned upon the author the other day more clearly than ever when a friend of his rushed into his office saying, ''I have been trying to see you for several days. I have just failed to get a job for which I had been working, and I am told that I cannot expect a promotion until I get my 'darkter's 'gree.' '' That is what he called it. He could not even pronounce the words, but he is determined to have his ''darkter's 'gree'' to get the job in sight.

This shameful status of higher education is due in a large measure to low standards of institutions with a tendency toward the diploma-mill procedure. To get a job or to hold one you go in and stay until they ''grind'' you out a ''darkter's 'gree.'' And you do not have to worry any further. The assumption is that almost any school will be glad to have you thereafter, and you will receive a large salary.

Investigation has shown, however, that men who have the doctorate not only lose touch with the common people, but they do not do as much creative work as those of less formal education. After having this honor conferred upon them, these so-called scholars often rest on their oars. Few persons have thought of the seriousness of such inertia among men who are put in the lead of things because of meeting statutory requirements of frontier universities which are not on the frontier.

The General Education Board and the Julius Rosenwald Fund have a policy which may be a partial solution of the undeveloped Negro college instructor's problem. These foundations are giving Negro teachers scholarships to improve themselves for work in the sphere in which they are now laboring in the South. These boards, as a rule, do not send one to school to work for the Doctor's degree. If they find a man of experience and good judgment, showing possibilities for growth, they will provide for him to study a year or more to refresh his mind with whatever there is new in his field. Experience has shown that teachers thus helped have later done much better work than Doctors of Philosophy made to order.

The Northern universities, moreover, cannot do graduate work for Negroes along certain lines when they are concentrating on the educational needs of people otherwise circumstanced.

The graduate school for Negroes studying chemistry is with George W. Carver at Tuskegee. At least a hundred youths should wait daily upon the words of this scientist to be able to pass on to the generations unborn his great knowledge of agricultural chemistry. Negroes desiring to specialize in agriculture should do it with workers like T. M. Campbell and B. F. Hubert among the Negro farmers of the South.

In education itself the situation is the same. Neither Columbia nor Chicago can give an advanced course in Negro rural education, for their work in education is based primarily upon what they know of the educational needs of the whites. Such work for Negroes must be done under the direction of the trail blazers who are building school houses and reconstructing the educational program of those in the backwoods. Leaders of this type can supply the foundation upon which a university of realistic education may be established.

We offer no argument here against earning advanced degrees, but these should come as honors conferred for training crowned with scholastic distinction, not to enable a man to increase his salary or find a better paying position. The schools which are now directing attention exclusively to these external marks of learning will not contribute much to the uplift of the Negro.

In Cleveland not long ago the author found

at the Western Reserve University something unusually encouraging. A native of Mississippi, a white man trained in a Northern university and now serving as a professor in one, has under him in sociology a Negro student from Georgia. For his dissertation this Negro is collecting the sayings of his people in everyday life—their morning greetings, their remarks about the weather, their comments on things which happen around them, their reactions to things which strike them as unusual, and their efforts to interpret life as the panorama passes before them. This white Mississippian and black Georgian are on the right way to understand the Negro and, if they do not fall out about social equality, they will serve the Negro much better than those who are trying to find out whether Henry VIII lusted more after Anne Boleyn than after Catherine of Aragon or whether Elizabeth was justly styled as more untruthful than Philip II of Spain.

CHAPTER V

THE greatest indictment of such education as Negroes have received, however, is that they have thereby learned little as to making a living, the first essential in civilization. Rural Negroes have always known something about agriculture, and in a country where land is abundant they have been able to make some sort of living on the soil even though they have not always employed scientific methods of farming. In industry where the competition is keener, however, what the Negro has learned in school has had little bearing on the situation, as pointed out above. In business the rôle of education as a factor in the uplift of the Negro has been still less significant. The Negroes of today are unable to employ one another, and the whites are inclined to call on Negroes only when workers of their own race have been taken care of. For the solution of this problem the "mis-educated" Negro has offered no remedy whatever.

What Negroes are now being taught does not bring their minds into harmony with life as they must face it. When a Negro student works his way through college by polishing shoes he does not think of making a special study of the science underlying the production and distribution of leather and its products that he may some day figure in this sphere. The Negro boy sent to college by a mechanic seldom dreams of learning mechanical engineering to build upon the foundation his father has laid, that in years to come he may figure as a contractor or a consulting engineer. The Negro girl who goes to college hardly wants to return to her mother if she is a washerwoman, but this girl should come back with sufficient knowledge of physics and chemistry and business administration to use her mother's work as a nucleus for a modern steam laundry. A white professor of a university recently resigned his position to become rich by running a laundry for Negroes in a Southern city. A Negro college instructor would have considered such a suggestion an insult. The so-called education of Negro college graduates leads them to throw away opportunities which they have and to go in quest of those which they do not find.

In the case of the white youth in this country, they can choose their courses more at random and still succeed because of numerous opportunities offered by their people, but even they show so much more wisdom than do Negroes. For example, a year or two after the author left Harvard he found out West a schoolmate who was studying wool. "How did you happen to go into this sort of thing?" the author inquired. His people, the former replied, had had some experience in wool, and in college he prepared for this work. On the contrary, the author studied Aristotle, Plato, Marsiglio of Padua, and Pascasius Rathbertus when he was in college. His friend who studied wool, however, is now independently rich and has sufficient leisure to enjoy the cultural side of life which his knowledge of the science underlying his business developed, but the author has to make his living by begging for a struggling cause.

An observer recently saw at the market near his office a striking example of this inefficiency of our system. He often goes over there at noon to buy a bit of fruit and to talk with a young woman who successfully conducts a fruit stand there in cooperation with her mother. Some years ago he tried to teach her in high school; but her memory was poor, and she could not understand what he was trying to do. She stayed a few weeks, smiling at the others who toiled, and finally left to assist her mother in business. She learned from her mother, however, how to make a living and be happy.

This observer was reminded of this young woman soon thereafter when there came to visit him a friend who succeeded in mastering everything taught in high school at that time and later distinguished himself in college. This highly educated man brought with him a complaint against life. Having had extreme difficulty in finding an opportunity to do what he is trained to do, he has thought several times of committing suicide. A friend encouraged this despondent man to go ahead and do it. The sooner the better. The food and air which he is now consuming may then go to keep alive some one who is in touch with life and able to grapple with its problems. This man has been educated away from the fruit stand.

This friend had been trying to convince this misfit of the unusual opportunities for the Negroes in business, but he reprimanded his adviser for urging him to take up such a task when most Negroes thus engaged have been failures.

"If we invest our money in some enterprise of our own," said he, "those in charge will misuse or misappropriate it. I have learned from my study of economics that we had just as well keep on throwing it away."

Upon investigation, however, it was discovered that this complainant and most others like him have never invested anything in any of the Negro enterprises, although they have tried to make a living by exploiting them. But they feel a bit guilty on this account, and when they have some apparent ground for fault-finding they try to satisfy their conscience which all but condemns them for their suicidal course of getting

41

all they can out of the race while giving nothing back to it.

Gossiping and scandal-mongering Negroes, of course, come to their assistance. Mis-educated by the oppressors of the race, such Negroes expect the Negro business man to fail anyway. They seize, then, upon unfavorable reports, exaggerate the situation, and circulate falsehoods throughout the world to their own undoing. You read such headlines as GREATEST NEGRO BUSINESS FAILS, NEGRO BANK ROBBED BY ITS OFFICERS, and THE TWILIGHT OF NEGRO BUSINESS. The mis-educated Negroes, then, stand by saying:

"I told you so. Negroes cannot run business. My professors pointed that out to me years ago when I studied economics in college; and I never intend to put any of my money in any Negro enterprise."

Yet, investigation shows that in proportion to the amount of capital invested Negro enterprises manifest about as much strength as businesses of others similarly situated. Negro business men have made mistakes, and they are still making them; but the weak link in the chain is that they are not properly supported and do not always grow strong enough to pass through a crisis. The Negro business man, then, has not failed so much as he has failed to get support of Negroes who should be mentally developed sufficiently to see the wisdom of supporting such enterprises.

Now the "highly educated" Negroes who have studied economics at Harvard, Yale, Columbia, and Chicago, will say that the Negro cannot succeed in business because their professors who have never had a moment's experience in this sphere have written accordingly. The whites, they say, have the control of the natural resources and so monopolize the production of raw materials as to eliminate the competition of the Negro. Apparently this is true. All things being equal from the point of view of the oppressor, he sees that the Negro cannot meet the test.

The impatient, "highly educated" Negroes, therefore, say that since under the present system of capitalism the Negro has no chance to toil upward in the economic sphere, the only hope for bettering his condition in this respect is through socialism, the overthrow of the present economic régime, and the inauguration of popular control of resources and agencies which are now being operated for personal gain. This thought is gaining ground among Negroes in this country, and it is rapidly sweeping them into the ranks of what are commonly known as "Communists."

There can be no objection to this radical change, if it brings with it some unselfish genius to do the task better than it is now being done under the present régime of competition. Russia so far has failed to do well this particular thing under a proletarian dictatorship in an

43

agricultural country. But whether this millennium comes or not, the capitalistic system is so strongly intrenched at present that the radicals must struggle many years to overthrow it; and if the Negro has to wait until that time to try to improve his condition he will be starved out so soon that he will not be here to tell the story. The Negro, therefore, like all other oppressed people, must learn to do the so-called "impossible."

The "uneducated" Negro business man, however, is actually at work doing the very thing which the "mis-educated" Negro has been taught to believe cannot be done. This much-handicapped Negro business man could do better if he had some assistance, but our schools are turning out men who do as much to impede the progress of the Negro in business as they do to help him. The trouble is that they do not think for themselves.

If the "highly educated" Negro would forget most of the untried theories taught him in school, if he could see through the propaganda which has been instilled into his mind under the pretext of education, if he would fall in love with his own people and begin to sacrifice for their uplift—if the "highly educated" Negro would do these things, he could solve some of the problems now confronting the race.

During recent years we have heard much of education in business administration departments in Negro colleges; but if they be judged by the products turned out by these departments they are not worth a "continental." The teachers in this field are not prepared to do the work, and the trustees of our institutions are spending their time with trifles instead of addressing themselves to the study of a situation which threatens the Negro with economic extermination.

Recently the author saw the need for a change of attitude when a young woman came almost directly to his office after her graduation from a business school to seek employment. After hearing her story he finally told her that he would give her a trial at fifteen dollars a week.

"Fifteen dollars a week!" she cried, "I cannot live on that, sir."

"I do not see why you cannot," he replied. "You have lived for some time already, and you say that you have never had permanent employment, and you have none at all now."

"But a woman has to dress and to pay board," said she; "and how can she do it on such a pittance?"

The amount offered was small, but it was a great deal more than she is worth at present. In fact, during the first six or nine months of her connection with some enterprise it will be of more service to her than she will be to the firm. Coming out of school without experience,

45

she will be a drag on a business until she learns to discharge some definite function in it. Instead of requiring the firm to pay her she should pay it for training her. Negro business today, then, finds the "mis-educated employees" its heaviest burden. Thousands of graduates of white business schools spend years in establishments in undergoing apprenticeship without pay and rejoice to have the opportunity thus to learn how to do things.

The schools in which Negroes are now being trained, however, do not give our young people this point of view. They may occasionally learn the elements of stenography and accounting, but they do not learn how to apply what they have studied. The training which they undergo gives a false conception of life when they believe that the business world owes them a position of leadership. They have the idea of business training that we used to have of teaching when it was thought that we could teach anything we had studied.

Graduates of our business schools lack the courage to throw themselves upon their resources and work for a commission. The large majority of them want to be sure of receiving a certain amount at the end of the week or month. They do not seem to realize that the great strides in business have been made by paying men according to what they do. Persons with such false impressions of life are not good representatives of schools of business administration.

Not long ago a firm of Washington, D. C., appealed to the graduates of several of our colleges and offered them an inviting proposition on the commission basis, but only five of the hundreds appealed to responded and only two of the five gave satisfaction. Another would have succeeded, but he was not honest in handling money because he had learned to purloin the treasury of the athletic organization while in college. All of the others, however, were anxious to serve somewhere in an office for a small wage a week.

Recently one of the large insurance companies selected for special training in this line fifteen college graduates of our accredited institutions and financed their special training in insurance. Only one of the number, however, rendered efficient service in this field. They all abandoned the effort after a few days' trial and accepted work in hotels and with the Pullman Company, or they went into teaching or something else with a fixed stipend until they could enter upon the practice of professions. The thought of the immediate reward, shortsightedness, and the lack of vision and courage to struggle and win the fight made them failures to begin with. They are unwilling to throw aside their coats and collars and do the groundwork of Negro business and thus make opportunities for themselves instead of begging others for a chance.

The educated Negro from the point of view of commerce and industry, then, shows no mental power to understand the situation which he finds. He has apparently read his race out of that sphere, and with the exception of what the illiterate Negroes can do blindly the field is left wide open for foreign exploitation. Foreigners see this opportunity as soon as they reach our shores and begin to manufacture and sell to Negroes especially such things as caps, neckties, and housedresses which may be produced at a small cost and under ordinary circumstances. The main problem with the Negro in this field, however, is salesmanship; that is where he is weak.

It is unfortunate, too, that the educated Negro does not understand or is unwilling to start small enterprises which make the larger ones possible. If he cannot proceed according to the methods of the gigantic corporations about which he reads in books, he does not know how to take hold of things and organize the communities of the poor along lines of small businesses. Such training is necessary, for the large majority of Negroes conducting enterprises have not learned business methods and do not understand the possibilities of the field in which they operate. Most of them in the beginning had had no experience, and started out with such

48

knowledge as they could acquire by observing some one's business from the outside. One of them, for example, had waited on a white business club in passing the members a box of cigars or bringing a pitcher of water. When they began to discuss business, however, he had to leave the room. About the only time he could see them in action was when they were at play, indulging in extravagances which the Negro learned to take up before he could afford them.

Negro businesses thus handicapped, therefore, have not developed stability and the capacity for growth. Practically all worth while Negro businesses which were flourishing in 1900 are not existing today. How did this happen? Well, Negro business men have too much to do. They have not time to read the business literature and study the market upon which they depend, and they may not be sufficiently trained to do these things. They are usually operating in the dark or by the hit-or-miss method. They cannot secure intelligent guidance because the schools are not turning out men properly trained to take up Negro business as it is to develop and make it what it ought to be rather than find fault with it. Too often when the founder dies, then, the business dies with him; or it goes to pieces soon after he passes away, for nobody has come into sufficiently close contact with him to learn the secret of his success in spite of his handicaps.

The business among Negroes, too, continues individualistic in spite of advice to the contrary. The founder does not take kindly to the co-operative plan, and such business education as we now give the youth does not make their suggestions to this effect convincing. If the founder happens to be unusually successful, too, the business may outgrow his knowledge, and becoming too unwieldy in his hands, may go to pieces by errors of judgment; or because of mismanagement it may go into the hands of whites who are usually called in at the last hour to do what they call refinancing but what really means the actual taking over of the business from the Negroes. The Negroes, then, finally withdraw their patronage because they realize that it is no longer an enterprise of the race, and the chapter is closed.

All of the failures of the Negro business, however, are not due to troubles from without. Often the Negro business man lacks common sense. The Negro in business, for example, too easily becomes a social ''lion.'' He sometimes plunges into the leadership in local matters. He becomes popular in restricted circles, and men of less magnetism grow jealous of his inroads. He learns how richer men of other races waste money. He builds a finer home than anybody else in the community, and in his social program he does not provide for much contact with the very people upon whom he must depend for patronage. He has the finest car, the most expensive dress, the best summer home, and so far outdistances his competitors in society that they often set to work in child-like fashion to bring him down to their level.

CHAPTER VI

ONE of the most striking evidences of the failure of higher education among Negroes is their estrangement from the masses, the very people upon whom they must eventually count for carrying out a program of progress. Of this the Negro churches supply the most striking illustration. The large majority of Negro communicants still belong to these churches, but the more education the Negroes undergo the less comfort they seem to find in these evangelical groups. These churches do not measure up to the standard set by the university preachers of the Northern centres of learning. Most Negroes returning as finished products from such institutions, then, are forever lost to the popular Negro churches. The unchurched of this class do not become members of such congregations, and those who have thus connected themselves remain chiefly for political or personal reasons and tend to become communicants in name only.

The Negro church, however, although not a shadow of what it ought to be, is the great asset of the race. It is a part of the capital that the race must invest to make its future. The Negro church has taken the lead in education in the schools of the race, it has supplied a forum for the thought of the "highly educated" Negro, it has originated a large portion of the business controlled by Negroes, and in many cases it has made it possible for Negro professional men to exist. It is unfortunate, then, that these classes do not do more to develop the institution. In thus neglecting it they are throwing away what they have, to obtain something which they think they need. In many respects, then, the Negro church during recent generations has become corrupt. It could be improved, but those Negroes who can help the institution have deserted it to exploiters, grafters, and libertines. The "highly educated" Negroes have turned away from the people in the churches, and the gap between the masses and the "talented tenth" is rapidly widening.

Of this many examples may be cited. When the author recently attended in Washington, D. C., one of the popular Negro churches with a membership of several thousands he saw a striking case in evidence. While sitting there he thought of what a power this group could become under the honest leadership of intelligent men and women. Social uplift, business, public welfare—all have their possibilities there if a score or more of our "highly educated" Negroes would work with these people at that center. Looking carefully throughout the audience for such persons, however, he recognized only two college graduates, Kelly Miller and himself; but the former had come to receive from the church a donation to the Community Chest, and the author had come according to appointment to make an appeal in behalf of Miss Nannie H. Burroughs' school. Neither one had manifested any interest in that particular church. This is the way most of them receive attention from our "talented tenth."

Some "highly educated" Negroes say that they have not lost their interest in religion, that they have gone into churches with a more intellectual atmosphere in keeping with their new thoughts and aspirations. And then there is a sort of contagious fever which takes away from the churches of their youth others of less formal education. Talking with a friend from Alabama, the other day, the author found out that after her father had died and she had moved to Washington she forsook the Baptist church in which he had been a prominent worker and joined a ritualistic church which is more fashionable.

Such a change of faith is all right in a sense, for no sensible person today would dare to make an argument in favor of any particular religion. Religion is but religion, if the people live up to the faith they profess. What is said here with respect to the popular churches of Negroes, which happen to be chiefly Methodist and Baptist, would hold also if they were mainly Catholic and Episcopal, provided the large majority of Negroes belonged to those churches. The point here is that the ritualistic churches into which these Negroes have gone do not touch the masses, and they show no promising future for racial development. Such institutions are controlled by those who offer the Negroes only limited opportunity and then sometimes on the condition that they be segregated in the court of the gentiles outside of the temple of Jehovah.

How an "educated Negro" can thus leave the church of his people and accept such jimcrowism has always been a puzzle. He cannot be a thinking man. It may be a sort of slave psychology which causes this preference for the leadership of the oppressor. The excuse sometimes given for seeking such religious leadership is that the Negro evangelical churches are "fogy," but a thinking man would rather be behind the times and have his self-respect than compromise his manhood by accepting segregation. They say that in some of the Negro churches bishoprics are actually bought, but it is better for the Negro to belong to a church where one can secure a bishopric by purchase than be a member of one which would deny the promotion on account of color.

With respect to developing the masses, then, the Negro race has lost ground in recent years. In 1880 when the Negroes had begun to make themselves felt in teaching, the attitude of the leaders was different from what it is today. At that time men went off to school to prepare themselves for the uplift of a downtrodden people. In our time too many Negroes go to school to memorize certain facts to pass examinations for jobs. After they obtain these positions they pay little attention to humanity. This attitude of the "educated Negro" toward the masses results partly from the general trend of all persons toward selfishness, but it works more disastrously among the Negroes than among the whites because the lower classes of the latter have had so much more opportunity.

For some time the author has been making a special study of the Negroes in the City of Washington to compare their condition of today with that of the past. Now although the "highly educated" Negroes of the District of Columbia have multiplied and apparently are in better circumstances than ever, the masses show almost as much backwardness as they did in 1880. Sometimes you find as many as two or three store-front churches in a single block where Negroes indulge in heathen-like practices which could hardly be equaled in the jungle. The Negroes in Africa have not descended to such depths. Although born and brought up in the Black Belt of the South the author never saw there such idolatrous tendencies as he has seen under the dome of the Capitol.

Such conditions show that the undeveloped Negro has been abandoned by those who should help him. The educated white man, said an observer recently, differs from the "educated Negro" who so readily forsakes the belated element of his race. When a white man sees persons of his own race tending downward to a level of disgrace he does not rest until he works out some plan to lift such unfortunates to higher ground; but the Negro forgets the delinquents of his race and goes his way to feather his own nest, as he has done in leaving the masses in the popular churches.

This is sad indeed, for the Negro church is the only institution the race controls. With the exception of the feeble efforts of a few all but starved-out institutions, the education of the Negroes is controlled by the other element; and save the dramatization of practical education by Booker T. Washington, Negroes have not influenced the system at all in America. In business, the lack of capital, credit, and experience has prevented large undertakings to accumulate the wealth necessary for the ease and comfort essential to higher culture.

In the church, however, the Negro has had sufficient freedom to develop this institution in his own way; but he has failed to do so. His religion is merely a loan from the whites who have enslaved and segregated the Negroes; and the organization, though largely an independent

Negro institution, is dominated by the thought of the oppressors of the race. The "educated" Negro minister is so trained as to drift away from the masses and the illiterate preachers into whose hands the people inevitably fall are unable to develop a doctrine and procedure of their own. The dominant thought is to make use of the dogma of the whites as means to an end. Whether the system is what it should be or not it serves the purpose.

In chameleon-like fashion the Negro has taken up almost everything religious which has come along instead of thinking for himself. The English split off from the Catholics because Henry VIII had difficulty in getting sanction from the Church to satisfy his lust for amorous women, and Negroes went with this ilk, singing "God save the King." Others later said the thing necessary is baptism by immersion; and the Negroes joined them as Baptists. Another circle of promoters next said we must have a new method of doing things and we shall call ourselves Methodists; and the Negroes, then, embraced that faith. The Methodists and Baptists split up further on account of the custom of holding slaves; and the Negroes arrayed themselves on the respective sides. The religious agitators divided still more on questions beyond human power to understand; and the Negroes started out in similar fashion to imitate them.

For example, thirty of the two hundred and thirteen religious bodies reported in 1926 were exclusively Negro, while thirty which were primarily white demoninations had one or more Negro churches among their number. In other words, Negroes have gone into practically all sects established by the whites; and, in addition to these, they have established thirty of their own to give the system further complication and subdivision. The situation in these churches is aggravated, too, by having too many ministers and about five times as many supervisory officials as a church embracing all Negro communicants would actually need. All of the Negro Methodists in the world, if united, would not need more than twelve bishops, and these would have time to direct the affairs of both Methodists and Baptists in a united church. There is no need for three or four bishops, each teaching the same faith and practice while duplicating the work of the other in the same area merely because a long time ago somebody following the ignorant oppressors of the race in these churches committed the sin of dissension and strife. For all of this unnecessary expense impoverished Negroes have to pay.

The "theology" of "foreigners," too, is the important factor in this disunion of churches and the burden which they impose on an unenlightened people. Theologians have been the "bane of bliss and source of woe." While bringing the joy of conquest to their own camp they have confused the world with disputes which have divided the church and stimulated division and subdivision to the extent that it no longer functions as a Christian agency for the uplift of all men.

To begin with, theology is of pagan origin. Albert Magnus and Thomas Aquinas worked out the first system of it by applying to religious discussion the logic of Aristotle, a pagan philosopher, who believed neither in the creation of the world nor the immortality of the soul. At best it was degenerate learning, based upon the theory that knowledge is gained by the mind working upon itself rather than upon matter or through sense perception. The world was, therefore, confused with the discussion of absurdities as it is today by those of prominent churchmen. By their peculiar "reasoning," too, theologians have sanctioned most of the ills of the ages. They justified the Inquisition, serfdom, and slavery. Theologians of our time defend segregation and the annihilation of one race by the other. They have drifted away from righteousness into an effort to make wrong seem to be right.

While we must hold the Negroes responsible for following these ignorant theorists, we should not charge to their account the origination of this nonsense with which they have confused thoughtless people. As said above, the

Negro has been so busy doing what he is told to do that he has not stopped long enough to think about the meaning of these things. He has borrowed the ideas of his traducers instead of delving into things and working out some thought of his own. Some Negro leaders of these religious factions know better, but they hold their following by keeping the people divided, in emphasizing nonessentials the insignificance of which the average man may not appreciate. The "highly educated" Negroes who know better than to follow these unprincipled men have abandoned these popular churches.

While serving as the avenue of the oppressor's propaganda, the Negro church, although doing some good, has prevented the union of diverse elements and has kept the race too weak to overcome foes who have purposely taught Negroes how to quarrel and fight about trifles until their enemies can overcome them. This is the keynote to the control of the so-called inferior races by the self-styled superior. The one thinks and plans while the other in excited fashion seizes upon and destroys his brother with whom he should cooperate.

CHAPTER VII

DISSENSION AND WEAKNESS

IN recent years the churches in enlightened centres have devoted less attention to dissension than formerly, but in the rural districts and small cities they have not changed much; and neither in urban communities nor in the country has any one succeeded in bringing these churches together to work for their general welfare. The militant sects are still fighting one another, and in addition to this the members of these sects are contending among themselves. The spirit of Christ cannot dwell in such an atmosphere.

Recent experiences show that these dissensions are about as rank as ever. For example, a rural community, in which an observer spent three weeks a year ago, has no church at all, although eight or ten families live there. No church can thrive among them because, with one or two exceptions, each family represents a different denomination, and the sectarian bias is so pronounced that one will not accept the procedure of the other. Each one loves his fellow man if he thinks as he does; but if his fellow man does not, he hates and shuns him.

In another rural community where the same observer recently spent two weeks he found a small and poorly attended Methodist church. Worshiping there one Sunday morning, he counted only four persons who lived in the community. Others might have come, for there was no other church for them in that place; but this particular church was not of their faith, and their number was too small to justify the establishment of one to their liking. The support given the unfortunate pastor there is so meager that he can hardly afford to come to them once a month, and consequently these peasants are practically without spiritual leadership. People who are so directed as to develop such an attitude are handicapped for life.

Some one recently inquired as to why the religious schools do not teach the people how to tolerate differences of opinion and to cooperate for the common good. This, however, is the thing which these institutions have refused to do. Religious schools have been established, but they are considered necessary to supply workers for denominational outposts and to keep alive the sectarian bias by which the Baptists hope to outstrip the Methodists or the latter the former. No teacher in one of these schools has advanced a single thought which has become a working principle in Christendom, and not one of these centres is worthy of the name of a school of theology. If one would bring together all of the teachers in such schools and carefully sift them he would not find in the whole group a sufficient number qualified to conduct one accredited school of religion. The large majority of them are engaged in imparting to the youth worn-out theories of the ignorant oppressor.

This lack of qualified teachers in Negro schools of theology, however, is not altogether the fault of the teachers themselves. It is due largely to the system to which they belong. Their schools of "theology" are impoverished by their unnecessary multiplication, and consequently the instructors are either poorly paid or not compensated at all. Many of them have to farm, conduct enterprises, or pastor churches to make a living while trying to teach. Often, then, only the inefficient can be retained under such circumstances. Yet those who see how they have failed because of these things nevertheless object to the unification of the churches as taught by Jesus of Nazareth, whom they have all but ceased to follow because of their sectarian bias obtained from thumb-worn books of misguided Americans and Europeans.

Recently an observer saw a result of this in the sermon of a Negro college graduate, trying to preach to a church of the masses. He referred to all the great men in the history of a certain country to show how religious they were, whether they were or not. When he undertook to establish the Christian character of Napoleon, however, several felt like leaving the place in disgust. The climax of the service was a prayer by another "mis-educated" Negro who devoted most of the time to thanking God for Cicero and Demosthenes. Here, then, was a case of the religion of the pagan handed down by the enslaver and segregationist to the Negro.

Returning from the table where he had placed his offering in a church on a Sunday morning not long thereafter, this observer saw another striking example of this failure to hit the mark. He stopped to inquire of his friend, Jim Minor, as to why he had not responded to the appeal for a collection.

"What!" said Jim, "I ain't givin' that man nothing. That man ain't fed me this morning, and I ain't feedin' him."

This was Jim's reaction to a "scholarly" sermon entitled "The Humiliation of the Incarnation." During the discourse, too, the minister had had much to say about John Knox Orthodox, and another of the communicants bowing at that shrine inquired of the observer later as to who this John Knox Orthodox was and where he lived. The observer could not answer all of the inquiries thus evoked, but he tried to explain the best he could that the speaker had "studied" history and theology.

This was the effect this sermon had on an earnest congregation. The minister had attended a school of theology but had merely memorized words and phrases, which meant little to him and nothing to those who heard his discourse. The school in which he had been trained followed the traditional course for ministers, devoting most of the time to dead languages and dead issues. He had given attention to polytheism, monotheism, and the doctrine of the Trinity. He had studied also the philosophical basis of the Caucasian dogma, the elements of that theology, and the schism by which fanatics made religion a football and multiplied wars only to moisten the soil of Europe with the blood of unoffending men.

This minister had given no attention to the religious background of the Negroes to whom he was trying to preach. He knew nothing of their spiritual endowment and their religious experience as influenced by their traditions and environment in which the religion of the Negro has developed and expressed itself. He did not seem to know anything about their present situation. These honest people, therefore, knew nothing additional when he had finished his discourse. As one communicant pointed out, their wants had not been supplied, and they wondered where they might go to hear a word which had some bearing upon the life which they had to live.

Not long ago when the author was in Virginia he inquired about a man who was once a popular preacher in that state. He is here, they said, but he is not preaching now. He went off to school, and when he came back the people could not understand what he was talking about. Then he began to find fault with the people because they would not come to church. He called them fogy, because they did not appreciate his new style of preaching and the things he talked about. The church went down to nothing, and he finally left it and took up farming.

In a rural community, then, a preacher of this type must fail unless he can organize separately members of the popular Methodist and Baptist churches who go into the ritualistic churches or establish certain "refined" Methodist or Baptist churches catering to the "talented tenth." For lack of adequate numbers, however, such churches often fail to develop sufficient force to do very much for themselves or for anybody else. On Sunday morning, then, their pastors have to talk to the benches. While these truncated churches go higher in their own atmosphere of self-satisfaction the mentally undeveloped are left to sink lower because of the lack of contact with the better trained. If the latter exercised a little more judgment, they would be able to influence these people for good by gradually introducing advanced ideas.

Because our "highly educated" people do not do this, large numbers of Negroes drift into

churches led by the "uneducated" ministers
who can scarcely read and write. These preachers do not know much of what is found in school
books and can hardly make use of a library in
working out a sermon; but they understand the
people with whom they deal, and they make
such use of the human laboratory that sometimes they become experts in solving vexing
problems and meeting social needs. They would
be much better preachers if they could have attended a school devoted to the development of
the mind rather than to cramming it with ex-
traneous matters which have no bearing on the
task which lies before them. Unfortunately,
however, very few of such schools of religion
now exist.

For lack of intelligent guidance, then, the
Negro church often fulfils a mission to the contrary of that for which it was established. Because the Negro church is such a free field and
it is controlled largely by the Negroes themselves, it seems that practically all the incom-
petents and undesirables who have been barred
from other walks of life by race prejudice and
economic difficulties have rushed into the ministry for the exploitation of the people. Honest
ministers who are trying to do their duty, then,
find their task made difficult by these men who
stoop to practically everything conceivable. Almost anybody of the lowest type may get into
the Negro ministry. The Methodists claim that

they have strict regulations to prevent this, but their net draws in proportionately as many undesirables as one finds among the Baptists.

As an evidence of the depths to which the institution has gone a resident of Cincinnati recently reported a case of its exploitation by a railroad man who lost his job and later all his earnings in a game in a den of vice in that city. To refinance himself he took an old black frock coat and a Bible and went into the heart of Tennessee, where he conducted at various points a series of distracted, protracted meetings which netted him two hundred and ninety-nine converts to the faith and four hundred dollars in cash. He was enabled thereby to return to the game in Cincinnati and he is still in the lead. Other such cases are frequently reported.

The large majority of Negro preachers of to-day, then, are doing nothing more than to keep up the mediæval hell-fire scare which the whites have long since abandoned to emphasize the humanitarian trend in religion through systematized education. The young people of the Negro race could be held in the church by some such program, but the Negro's Christianity does not conceive of social uplift as a duty of the church; and consequently Negro children have not been adequately trained in religious matters to be equal to the social demands upon them. Turning their back on mediævalism, then, these untrained youth think nothing of

taking up moonshining, gambling, and rack-
eteering as occupations; and they find great
joy in smoking, drinking, and fornication as
diversions. They cannot accept the old ideas,
and they do not understand the new.

What the Negro church is, however, has been
determined largely by what the white man has
taught the race by precept and example. We
must remember that the Negroes learned their
religion from the early white Methodists and
Baptists who evangelized the slaves and the
poor whites when they were barred from prose-
lyting the aristocracy. The American white
people themselves taught Negroes to specialize
unduly in the "Praise the Lord," "Halleluiah"
worship. In the West Indies among the
Anglicans and among the Latin people Negroes
do not show such emotionalism. They are cold
and conservative.

Some of the American whites, moreover, are
just as far behind in this respect as are the
Negroes who have had less opportunity to learn
better. While in Miami, Florida, not long ago
the author found in two interracial "Holiness
Churches" that the following was a third or
fourth white. The whites joined whole-heartedly
with the Negroes in their "holy rolling" and
some of them seemed to be "rollers not holy."

A few months ago in Huntington, West Virginia, where the author was being entertained
by friends, the party was disturbed through-

out the evening by the most insane outbursts of white worshippers in a "Church of God" across the street. There they daily indulged in such whooping and screaming in "unknown tongues" that the Negroes have had to report them to the police as a nuisance. The author has made a careful study of the Negro church, but he has never known Negroes to do anything to surpass the performance of those heathen.

The American Negroes' ideas of morality, too, were borrowed from their owners. The Negroes could not be expected to raise a higher standard than their aristocratic governing class that teemed with sin and vice. This corrupt state of things did not easily pass away. The Negroes have never seen any striking examples among the whites to help them in matters of religion. Even during the colonial period the whites claimed that their ministers sent to the colonies by the Anglican Church, the progenitor of the Protestant Episcopal Church in America, were a degenerate class that exploited the people for money to waste it in racing horses and drinking liquor. Some of these ministers were known to have illicit relations with women and, therefore, winked at the sins of the officers of their churches, who sold their own offspring by slave women.

Although the author was born ten years after the Civil War the morals and religion of that régime continued even into his time. Many of the rich or well-to-do white men belonging to the churches in Buckingham County, Virginia, indulged in polygamy. They raised one family by a white woman and another by a colored or poor white woman. Both the owner of the largest slate quarry and the proprietor of the largest factory in that county lived in this fashion. One was an outstanding Episcopalian and the other a distinguished Catholic.

One day the foreman of the factory, a polygamous deacon of the local white Baptist Church, called the workmen together at noon for a short memorial service in honor of Parson Taylor, for almost half a century the pastor of the large white Baptist church in that section. The foreman made some remarks on the life of the distinguished minister, and then all sang "Shall We Meet Beyond the River?" But "to save his life" the author could not restrain himself from wondering all that time whether the foreman's white wife or colored paramour would greet him on the other side, and what a conflict there would be if they happened to get into an old-fashioned hair-pulling. In spite of his libertine connections, however, this foreman believed that he was a Christian, and when he died his eulogist commended his soul to God.

Some years later when the author was serving his six years' apprenticeship in the West Virginia coal mines he found at Nutallburg a very faithful vestryman of the white Episcopal

Church at that point. He was one of the most devout from the point of view of his co-workers. Yet, privately, this man boasted of having participated in that most brutal lynching of the four Negroes who thus met their doom at the hands of an angry mob in Clifton Forge, Virginia, in 1892.

It is very clear, then, that if Negroes got their conception of religion from slaveholders, libertines, and murderers, there may be something wrong about it, and it would not hurt to investigate it. It has been said that the Negroes do not connect morals with religion. The historian would like to know what race or nation does such a thing. Certainly the whites with whom the Negroes have come into contact have not done so.

CHAPTER VIII

IN the training for professions other than
the ministry and teaching the Negro has not
had full sway. Any extensive comment on professional education by the Negro, then, must be
mainly negative. We have not had sufficient
professional schools upon which we can base
an estimate of what the Negro educator can
do in this sphere. If mistakes have been made
in mis-educating the Negro professionally it
must be charged not so much to the account of
the Negroes themselves as to that of their
friends who have performed this task. We are
dealing here, then, mainly with information obtained from the study of Negroes who have been
professionally trained by whites in their own
schools and in mixed institutions.

The largest numbers of Negroes in professions other than the ministry or education are
physicians, dentists, pharmacists, lawyers and
actors. The numbers in these and other lines
have not adequately increased because of the
economic status of the Negroes and probably
because of a false conception of the rôle of the
professional man in the community and its re-

74

lation to him. The people whom the Negro professional men have volunteered to serve have not always given them sufficient support to develop that standing and solidarity which will make their position professional and influential. Most whites in contact with Negroes, always the teachers of their brethren in black, both by precept and practice, have treated the professions as aristocratic spheres to which Negroes should not aspire. We have had, then, a much smaller number than those who under different circumstances would have dared to cross the line; and those that did so were starved out by the whites who would not treat them as a professional class. This made it impracticable for Negroes to employ them in spheres in which they could not function efficiently. For example, because of a law that a man could not be admitted to the bar in Delaware without practicing a year under some lawyer in the state (and no white lawyer would grant a Negro such an opportunity until a few years ago) it was only recently that a Negro was admitted there.

Negroes, then, learned from their oppressors to say to their children that there were certain spheres into which they should not go because they would have no chance therein for development. In a number of places young men were discouraged and frightened away from certain professions by the poor showing made by those trying to function in them. Few had the courage to face this ordeal; and some professional schools in institutions for Negroes were closed about thirty or forty years ago, partly on this account.

This was especially true of the law schools, closed during the wave of legislation against the Negro, at the very time the largest possible number of Negroes needed to know the law for the protection of their civil and political rights. In other words, the thing which the patient needed most to pass the crisis was taken from him that he might more easily die. This one act among many others is an outstanding monument to the stupidity or malevolence of those in charge of Negro schools, and it serves as a striking demonstration of the mis-education of the race.

Almost any observer remembers distinctly the hard trials of the Negro lawyers. A striking example of their difficulties was supplied by the case of the first to be permanently established in Huntington, West Virginia. The author had entrusted to him the matter of correcting an error in the transfer of some property purchased from one of the most popular white attorneys in the state. For six months this simple transaction was delayed, and the Negro lawyer could not induce the white attorney to act. The author finally went to the office himself to complain of the delay. The white attorney frankly declared that he had not taken up the matter because he did not care to treat with a Negro attorney; but he would deal with the author, who happened to be at that time the teacher of a Negro school, and was, therefore, in his place.

At one time the Negroes in medicine and correlated fields were regarded in the same light. They had difficulty in making their own people believe that they could cure a complaint, fill a tooth, or compound a prescription. The whites said that they could not do it; and, of course, if the whites said so, it was true, so far as most Negroes were concerned. In those fields, however, actual demonstrations to the contrary have convinced a sufficient number of both Negroes and whites that such an attitude toward these classes is false, but there are many Negroes who still follow those early teachings, especially the "highly educated" who in school have been given the "scientific" reasons for it. It is a most remarkable process that while in one department of a university a Negro may be studying for a profession, in another department of the same university he is being shown how the Negro professional man cannot succeed. Some of the "highly educated," then, give their practice to those who are often inferior to the Negroes whom they thus pass by. Although there has been an increase in these particular spheres, however, the professions among

Negroes, with the exception of teaching and preaching, are still undermanned.

In the same way the Negro was once discouraged and dissuaded from taking up designing, drafting, architecture, engineering and chemistry. The whites, they were told, will not employ you and your people cannot provide such opportunities. The thought of pioneering or of developing the Negro to the extent that he might figure in this sphere did not dawn on those monitors of the Negroes preparing for their life's work. This tradition is still a heavy load in Negro education, and it forces many Negroes out of spheres in which they might function into those for which they may not have any aptitude.

In music, dramatics and correlated arts, too, the Negro has been unfortunately misled. Because the Negro is gifted as a singer and can render more successfully than others the music of his own people, he has been told that he does not need training. Scores of those who have undertaken to function in this sphere without adequate education, then, have developed only to a certain point beyond which they have not had ability to go. We cannot easily estimate how popular Negro musicians and their music might have become had they been taught to the contrary.

Of these, several instances may be cited. A distinguished man, talking recently as a member of a large Episcopal church, which maintains a Negro mission, mentioned his objection to the budget of fifteen hundred dollars a year for music for these segregated communicants. Inasmuch as the Negroes were naturally gifted in music he did not believe that any expensive training or direction was required. The small number of Negro colleges and universities which undertake the training of the Negro in music is further evidence of the belief that the Negro is all but perfect in this field and should direct his attention to the traditional curricula.

The same misunderstanding with respect to the Negro in dramatics is also evident. We have long had the belief that the Negro is a natural actor who does not require any stimulus for further development. In this assertion is the idea that because the Negro is good at dancing, joking, minstrelsy and the like he is "in his place" when "cutting a shine" and does not need to be trained to function in the higher sphere of dramatics. Thus misled, large numbers of Negroes ambitious for the stage have not bloomed forth into great possibilities. Too many of them have finally ended with rôles in questionable cafés, cabarets, and night clubs of America and Europe; and instead of increasing the prestige of the Negro they have brought the race into disgrace.

We scarcely realize what a poor showing we

79

make in dramatics in spite of our natural aptitude in this sphere. Only about a half dozen Negro actors have achieved greatness, but we have more actors and showmen than any other professionals except teachers and ministers. Where are these thousands of men and women in the histrionic sphere? What do we hear of them? What have they achieved? Their record shows that only a few measure up to the standard of the modern stage. Most of these would-be artists have no preparation for the tasks undertaken.

A careful study of the Negro in dramatics shows that only those who have actually taken the time to train themselves as they should be have finally endured. Their salvation has been to realize that adequate training is the surest way to attain artistic maturity. And those few who have thus understood the situation clearly demonstrate our ineptitude in the failure to educate the Negroes along the lines in which they could have admirably succeeded. Some of our schools have for some time undertaken this work as imitators of institutions dealing with persons otherwise circumstanced. Desirable results, therefore, have not followed, and the Negro on the stage is still mainly the product of the trial and error method.

Several other reasons may be given for the failure of a larger number of Negro actors to reach a higher level. In the first place, they have been recognized by the white man only in purely plantation comedy and minstrelsy, and because of the large number entering the field it has failed to offer a bright future for many of such aspirants. Repeatedly told by the white man that he could not function as an actor in a different sphere, the American Negro has all but ceased to attempt anything else. The successful career of Ira Aldridge in Shakespeare was forgotten until recently recalled by the dramatic success of Paul Robeson in Othello. The large majority of Negroes have settled down, then, to contentment as ordinary clowns and comedians. They have not had the courage or they have not learned how to break over the unnatural barriers and occupy higher ground.

The Negro author is no exception to the traditional rule. He writes, but the white man is supposed to know more about everything than the Negro. So who wants a book written by a Negro about one? As a rule, not even a Negro himself, for if he is really "educated," he must show that he has the appreciation for the best in literature. The Negro author, then, can neither find a publisher nor a reader; and his story remains untold. The Negro editors and reporters were once treated the same way, but thanks to the uneducated printers who founded most of our newspapers which have succeeded, these men of vision have made it possible for the "educated" Negroes to make a living in this sphere in proportion as they recover from their education and learn to deal with the Negro as he is and where he is.

CHAPTER IX

SOME time ago when Congressman Oscar De Priest was distributing by thousands copies of the Constitution of the United States certain wiseacres were disposed to make fun of it. What purpose would such an act serve? These critics, however, probably did not know that thousands and thousands of Negro children in this country are not permitted to use school books in which are printed the Declaration of Independence or the Constitution of the United States. Thomas Jefferson and James Madison are mentioned in their history as figures in politics rather than as expounders of liberty and freedom. These youths are not permitted to learn that Jefferson believed that government should derive its power from the consent of the governed.

Not long ago a measure was introduced in a certain State Legislature to have the Constitution of the United States thus printed in school histories, but when the bill was about to pass it was killed by some one who made the point that it would never do to have Negroes study the Constitution of the United States. If the

Negroes were granted the opportunity to peruse this document, they might learn to contend for the rights therein guaranteed; and no Negro teacher who gives attention to such matters of the government is tolerated in those backward districts. The teaching of government or the lack of such instruction, then, must be made to conform to the policy of "keeping the Negro in his place."

In like manner, the teaching of history in the Negro area has had its political significance. Starting out after the Civil War, the opponents of freedom and social justice decided to work out a program which would enslave the Negroes' mind inasmuch as the freedom of body had to be conceded. It was well understood that if by the teaching of history the white man could be further assured of his superiority and the Negro could be made to feel that he had always been a failure and that the subjection of his will to some other race is necessary the freedman, then, would still be a slave. If you can control a man's thinking you do not have to worry about his action. When you determine what a man shall think you do not have to concern yourself about what he will do. If you make a man feel that he is inferior, you do not have to compel him to accept an inferior status, for he will seek it himself. If you make a man think that he is justly an outcast, you do not have to order him to the back door. He will go without being told; and if there is no back door, his very nature will demand one.

This program, so popular immediately after the Civil War, was not new, but after this upheaval, its execution received a new stimulus. Histories written elsewhere for the former slave area were discarded, and new treatments of local and national history in conformity with the recrudescent propaganda were produced to give whites and blacks the biased point of view of the development of the nation and the relations of the races. Special treatments of the Reconstruction period were produced in apparently scientific form by propagandists who went into the first graduate schools of the East to learn modern historiography about half a century ago. Having the stamp of science, the thought of these polemics was accepted in all seats of learning. These rewriters of history fearlessly contended that slavery was a benevolent institution; the masters loved their slaves and treated them humanely; the abolitionists meddled with the institution which the masters eventually would have modified; the Civil War brought about by "fanatics" like William Lloyd Garrison and John Brown was unnecessary; it was a mistake to make the Negro a citizen, for he merely became worse off by incurring the displeasure of the master class that will never tolerate him as an equal; and the Negro must live in this country in a state of recognized inferiority.

Some of these theories may seem foolish, but historians even in the North have been won to this point of view. They ignore the recent works of Miss Elizabeth Donnan, Mrs. H. T. Catterall, and Dr. Frederic Bancroft, who have spent years investigating slavery and slave-trading. These are scientific productions with the stamp of the best scholarship in America, treatises produced from such genuine documents as the court records of the slaveholding section itself, and these authors have rendered the public a valuable service in removing the whitewash which pseudo-historians have been giving to slavery and slaveholders for more than a century.

In the preparation of Negroes, many of whom teach in the South, these biased Northern historians even convert them to such a faith. A few years ago the author happened to listen to a conversation of Negro lawyers in one of our Southern cities, in which they unanimously conceded practically every contention set forth in this program of propaganda. They denounced, therefore, all reconstructionists who advocated equality and justice for all. These Negroes had the biased point of view of the rewriters like Claude Bowers and had never been directed to the real history of that drama as set forth by A. A. Taylor, Francis B. Simkins and Robert

H. Woody of the new Southern school of thought. These Negro critics were especially hard on Negroes of our day who engage in agitation for actual democracy. Negroes themselves in certain parts join with the whites, then, in keeping out of the schools teachers who may be bold enough to teach the truth as it is. They usually say the races here are getting along amicably now, and we do not want these peaceful relations disturbed by the teaching of new political thought.

What they mean to say with respect to the peaceful relation of the races, then, is that the Negroes have been terrorized to the extent that they are afraid even to discuss political matters publicly. There must be no exposition of the principles of government in the schools, and this must not be done in public among Negroes with a view to stimulating political activity. Negroes engaged in other spheres in such communities finally come to the point of accepting silence on these matters as a fixed policy. Knowing that action to the contrary means mob rule which may destroy the peace and property of the community, they constitute themselves a sort of a vigilant committee to direct their fellows accordingly.

A few years ago a rather youthful looking high school principal in one of the large cities was unceremoniously dismissed because he said jocosely to the president of the board of education, in reply to his remark about his youthful bearing, "I am old enough to vote." "Horrors!" said the infuriated official. "Put him out. We brought him here to teach these Negroes how to work, and here he is thinking about voting." A few prominent Negroes of the place muttered a little, but they did nothing effective to correct this injustice.

In certain parts, therefore, the Negroes under such terrorism have ceased to think of political matters as their sphere. Where such things come into the teaching in more advanced work they are presented as matters of concern to a particular element rather than as functions in which all citizens may participate. The result is that Negroes grow up without knowledge of political matters which should concern all elements. To prevent the Negroes from learning too much about these things the whites in the schools are sometimes neglected also, but the latter have the opportunity to learn by contact, close observation, and actual participation in the affairs of government.

Negroes in certain parts, then, have all but abandoned voting even at points where it might be allowed. In some cases not as many as two thousand Negroes vote in a whole state. By special legislation providing for literacy tests and the payment of taxes their number of voters has been reduced to a negligible quantity, and the few who can thus function do not do so because they are often counted out when they have the deciding vote.

The tests established for the restriction of suffrage were not intended to stimulate political education but to eliminate the Negro vote by subterfuge. Negroes presenting themselves for registration are asked to do the all but impossible thing of expounding parts of the Constitution which have baffled high courts; but whites are asked simple questions which almost any illiterate man can answer. In this way the Negroes, however intelligent, are turned down; and all ignorant whites are permitted to vote. These laws, then, have retarded rather than stimulated the political education of both races. Such knowledge is apparently useless for Negroes and unnecessary for the whites, for the Negroes do not immediately profit by having it and the whites may function as citizens without it.

The effect of such a one-sided system is decidedly bad. One does not realize it until he talks with men and women of these districts, who because of the denial of these privileges have lost interest in political matters. A book agent working in the plantation area of Mississippi tested the knowledge of Negroes of these matters by asking them questions about the local and State government. He discovered that they knew practically nothing in this sphere. It was difficult to find any who knew who was president of the United States. One meets teachers, physicians, and ministers who do not know the ordinary operations of courts, the functions of the counsel, jury or judge, unless such knowledge has come by the bitter experience of having been imposed upon by some tribunal of injustice. Some of the "educated" Negroes do not pay attention to such important matters as the assessment of property and the collection of taxes, and they do not inform themselves as to how these things are worked out. An influential Negro in the South, then, is one who has nothing to do or say about politics and advises others to follow the same course.

The elimination of the Negro from politics, then, has been most unfortunate. The whites may have profited thereby temporarily, but they showed very little foresight. How the whites can expect to make of the Negroes better citizens by leading them to think that they should have no part in the government of this country is a mystery. To keep a man above vagabondage and crime he needs among other things the stimulus of patriotism, but how can a man be patriotic when the effect of his education is to the contrary?

What little chance the Negro has to learn by participation in politics in most parts of the South is unfortunately restricted now to corruption. The usual stir about electing delegates to the National Republican Convention from

the Southern States and the customary combat
the Negroes have with Lily-white corruptionists are about all the political matters which
claim their attention in the Lower South.
Neither the white nor the black faction, as a
rule, makes any effort to restore suffrage to
Negroes. The objective is merely the control
of delegates and Federal patronage for the
financial considerations involved. To do this
they resort to numerous contests culminating in
closing hotels and bolting doors for secret meetings. Since this is the only activity in which
Negroes can participate they have learned to
look upon it as honorable. Large numbers of
Negroes become excited over the contest and
give much publicity to it on the rostrum and in
the press as a matter of great importance. The
methods of these corruptionists of both races,
however, should be condemned as a disgrace to
the state and nation.

Instead of doing something to get rid of this
ilk, however, we find the "highly educated"
Negroes trying to plunge also into the mire.
One of the most discouraging aspects in Negro
life recently observed was that of a presidential
campaign. Prominent Negroes connected with
three of our leading institutions of learning
temporarily abandoned their work to round up
Negro votes for one of the candidates. The
objective, of course, was to control the few ordinary jobs which are allotted to Negro politicians

for their campaign services. When the successful candidate had been inaugurated, however, he carefully ignored them in the make-up of the personnel of his administration and treated Negroes in general with contempt. When you think of the fact that the Negroes who are being thus used are supposedly the most reputable Negro leaders and our most highly educated men you have to wonder whether the Negro has made any progress since Emancipation. The only consolation one can get out of it is that they may not represent the whole race.

In the North the Negroes have a better chance to acquire knowledge of political matters of the simple kind, but the bosses do not think it is advisable to enlighten them thoroughly. Negroes in parts are employed in campaigns, but they are not supposed to discuss such issues of the day as free trade, tariff for protection, the World Court, and the League of Nations. These Negro workers are supposed to tell their people how one politician seeking office has appointed more Negro messengers or charwomen in the service than the other or how the grandfather of the candidate stood with Lincoln and Grant through their ordeal and thus brought the race into its own. Another important task of these Negroes thus employed is also to abuse the opposing party, showing how hostile it has been to the Negro while the highly favorable party was doing so much for the race.

The course of these bosses has been interesting. At first the white man used the Negro leader by giving him a drink ocassionally. The next step was to give him sufficient money to set up drinks in the name of the white candidate. When drinking at the expense of the candidate became too common the politicians fell back on the distribution of funds in small amounts. When this finally proved to be insufficient, however, the politicians had to go a bit further and provide Jim Crow jobs in certain backrooms with the understanding that the functions of the so-called office would be merely nominal and the incumbents would have no close contact with white people. In this stage the Negroes find themselves today.

The undesirable aspect of the affair is that the Negro in spite of the changes from one method of approach to that of another is never brought into the inner circle of the party with which he is affiliated. He is always kept on the outside and is used as a means to an end. To obtain the meager consideration which he receives the Negro must work clandestinely through the back door. It has been unnecessary for the white man to change this procedure, for until recent years he has generally found it possible to satisfy the majority of Negroes with the few political positions earmarked as "Negro jobs" and to crush those who clamor for more recognition.

It is unfortunate, too, that such a large number of Negroes do not know any better than to stake their whole fortune on politics. History does not show that any race, especially a minority group, has ever solved an important problem by relying altogether on one thing, certainly not by parking its political strength on one side of the fence because of empty promises. There are Negroes who know better, but such thinkers are kept in the background by the traducers of the race to prevent the enlightenment of the masses. The misleading politicians are the only persons through whom the traducers act with respect to the Negro, and there are always a sufficient number of mentally undeveloped voters who will supply them a large following.

Even the few Negroes who are elected to office are often similarly uninformed and show a lack of vision. They have given little attention to the weighty problems of the nation; and in the legislative bodies to which they are elected, they restrict themselves as a rule to matters of special concern to the Negroes themselves, such as lynching, segregation and disfranchisement, which they have well learned by experience. This indicates a step backwards, for the Negroes who sat in Congress and in the State Legislatures during the Reconstruction worked for the enactment of measures of concern to all elements of the population regardless of color. Historians have not yet forgot what those Negro statesmen did in advocating public education, internal improvements, labor arbitration, the tariff, and the merchant marine.

CHAPTER X

HISTORY shows, then, that as a result of these unusual forces in the education of the Negro he easily learns to follow the line of least resistance rather than battle against odds for what real history has shown to be the right course. A mind that remains in the present atmosphere never undergoes sufficient development to experience what is commonly known as thinking. No Negro thus submerged in the ghetto, then, will have a clear conception of the present status of the race or sufficient foresight to plan for the future; and he drifts so far toward compromise that he loses moral courage. The education of the Negro, then, becomes a perfect device for control from without. Those who purposely promote it have every reason to rejoice, and Negroes themselves exultingly champion the cause of the oppressor.

A comparison of the record of the spokesmen of the race today with that of those of the eighteenth century shows a moral surrender. During the prolonged struggle between the French and English in America the Negroes held the balance of power at several strategic points and used it accordingly; today the Negro finds himself inconsequential because he can be parked on one side of the fence. The same balance of power was evident also during the American Revolution when Negro soldiers insisted on serving side by side with others; today many Negroes are content as menials in the army. At that time Negroes preached to mixed congregations; today we find Negroes busy separating them. The eighteenth-century Negro resented any such thing as social distinctions; today Negroes are saying that they do not want social equality. Negroes of that epoch said with the ancient poet, "I am a man and deem nothing that relates to man a matter of indifference to me"; today, however, the average Negro says, "Now, I am a colored man, and you white folks must settle that matter among yourselves."

At a still later date the American Negro showed more courage than he does today with all of his so-called enlightenment. When the free Negroes were advised a hundred years ago to go to Africa they replied that they would never separate themselves from the slave population of this country as they were brethren by the "ties of consanguinity, of suffering, and of wrong." Today, however, the Negro in the North turns up his nose at the crude migrant from the South who brings to the North the race problem but along with it more thrift and actual progress than the Northern Negro ever dreamed of.

When, again in 1816, free Negroes like Richard Allen, James Forten, and Robert Purvis, were referred to as a foreign element whose social status might not be secure in this country, instead of permitting the colonizationists to shove them aside as criminals to be deported to a distant shore, they replied in no uncertain terms that this soil in America which gave them birth is their only true home. "Here their fathers fought, bled, and died for this country and here they intended to stay." Today when such things come up you find Negroes appearing upon the scene to see how much pay they can obtain to assist in the proposed undoing of the race.

Further emphasizing this thought of resistance a few years later, Nathaniel Paul, a Baptist preacher of Albany, informed the colonizationists that the free Negroes would not permit their traducers to formulate a program for the race. You may go ahead with your plan to deport this element in order to make slavery secure, he warned; but the free Negroes will never emigrate to Africa. "We shall stay here and fight until the foul monster is crushed. Slavery must go."

"Did I believe it would always continue," said he, "and that man to the end of time would be permitted with impunity to usurp the same undue authority over his fellow, I would disavow any allegiance or obligation I was under to my fellow creatures, or any submission that I owed to the laws of my country! I would deny the superintending power of divine Providence in the affairs of this life; I would ridicule the religion of the Savior of the world, and treat as the worst of men the ministers of the everlasting gospel; I would consider my Bible as a book of false and delusive fables, and commit it to the flames; nay, I would still go farther; I would at once confess myself an atheist, and deny the existence of a holy God.''

And these Negroes of a century ago stood their ground and fought the pro-slavery deportationists to a standstill, for with the exception of a few pioneers the emigrants to Liberia were largely slaves manumitted on the condition that they would settle in Africa. These freedmen, then, could have no ideals but those of the slaveholding section from which they were sent. They established, therefore, a slavocracy in Liberia. If Liberia has failed, then, it is no evidence of the failure of the Negro in government. It is merely evidence of the failure of slavery.

The Negroes attacking Jim-Crowism almost a century ago fearlessly questioned the constitutionality of such a provision. Speaking through Charles Lenox Remond of that day, they said, ''There is a distinction between social and civil rights. We all claim the privilege of selecting our society and associations, but, in civil rights, one man has not the prerogative to define rights for another. These [race] distinctions react in all their wickedness—to say nothing of their concocted and systematized odiousness and absurdity—upon those who are illiberal and mean enough to practice them.''

In our day, however, we find some ''highly educated'' Negroes approving such Jim-Crowism. For example, not many years ago an outstanding Baptist preacher, dabbling in politics in West Virginia, suggested to the whites that they enact a Jim Crow car law in that State, and we had difficulty in crushing that sentiment. A few years thereafter the author heard one of our bishops say that we should not object to such separation, for we want to be by ourselves. When this distinguished churchman died the traducers of the Negro lauded him to the skies; and thoughtless members of the race, thinking that he deserved it, joined in the loud acclaim.

In this way the large majority of ''educated'' Negroes in the United States have accepted segregation and have become its fearless champions. Their filled but undeveloped minds do not enable them to understand that, although an opiate furnishes temporary relief, it does not remove the cause of the pain. In this case we have yielded on principle to satisfy the mob, but have not yet found an ultimate solution of the problem at hand. In our so-called democracy we are accustomed to give the majority what they want rather than educate them to understand what is best for them. We do not show the Negro how to overcome segregation, but we teach him how to accept it as final and just.

Numerous results from this policy may be cited. The white laboring man refuses to work with Negroes because of the false tradition that the Negro is an inferior, and at the same time the Negro for the same reason becomes content with menial service and drudgery. The politician excludes the Negro from the councils of his party and from the government because he has been taught that such is necessary to maintain the supremacy of his race; the Negro, trained in the same school of thought, accepts this as final and contends for such meager consideration as the bosses may begrudgingly grant him. An irate resident in an exclusive district protests against an invasion by Negroes because he has learned that these poverty-stricken people are carriers of disease and agents of crime; the Negroes, believing that such is the truth, remain content in the ghetto. The irrational parent forces the separation of the races in some schools because his child must occupy a seat next to a pupil of ''tainted'' African blood; the educated Negro accepts this as inevitable and welcomes the makeshift for his people. Children of Negroes are excluded from the playgrounds because of the assertion that they will contaminate those of the whites; the Negroes yielding, settle down to a policy of having their children grow up in neglected fashion in the most undesirable part of the city. The Negro is forced to ride in a Jim Crow car to stamp upon him more easily the badge of his "inferiority"; the "educated Negro" accepts it as settled and abandons the fight against this social proscription.

And thus goes segregation which is the most far-reaching development in the history of the Negro since the enslavement of the race. In fact, it is a sequel of slavery. It has been made possible by our system of mis-educating innocent people who did not know what was happening. It is so subtle that men have participated in promoting it without knowing what they were doing.

There are a few defenders of segregation who are doubtless sincere. Although nominally free they have never been sufficiently enlightened to see the matter other than as slaves. One can cite cases of Negroes who opposed emancipation and denounced the abolitionists. A few who became free reenslaved themselves. A still larger number made no effort to become free because they did not want to disconnect themselves from their masters, and their kind still object to full freedom.

Ever since the Civil War when Negroes were

first given a chance to participate in the management of their affairs they have been inconsistent and compromising. They have tried to gain one thing on one day by insisting on equality for all, while at the same time endeavoring to gain another point the next day by segregation. At one moment Negroes fight for the principle of democracy, and at the very next moment they barter it away for some temporary advantage. You cannot have a thing and dispose of it at the same time.

For example, the Negro political leaders of the Reconstruction period clamored for suffrage and the right of holding office, serving in the militia, and sitting on the jury; but few of them wanted white and colored children to attend the same school. When expressing themselves on education most of them took the position of segregationists; and Charles Sumner in his fight for the civil rights of the Negro had to eliminate mixed schools from his program not only because many whites objected but also because the Negroes themselves did not seem to want them. All of these leaders might not have been looking for jobs in those days; but as nominal freemen, who were still slaves, they did not feel comfortable in the presence of their former masters.

These timorous men were very much like some Negroes who were employed near the author's home in Virginia by a Northern farmer, who had moved into the State after the Civil War. When breakfast time came the first morning he called them in to eat at the table with his family. These actual slaves, however, immediately lost their appetite. One finally called the employer aside and settled the matter in another way. He said:

"Now boss, you ain't used to de rules ob dis country. We just can't sit at de table wid wite folks. We been use ter eating a cake er bread out yonder 'tween de plow handles. Les us go out dar."

The system, therefore, has extended from one thing to another until the Negroes today find themselves hedged in by the color bar almost every way they turn; and, set off by themselves, the Negroes cannot learn from the example of others with whom they might come into contact. In the ghetto, too, they are not permitted to construct and carry out a program of their own. These segregating institutions interfere with the development of self-help among Negroes, for often Negroes fail to raise money to establish institutions which they might control, but they readily contribute large sums for institutions which segregate persons of African blood.

Denied participation in the higher things of life, the "educated" Negro himself joins, too, with ill-designing persons to handicap his people by systematized exploitation. Feeling that

104

the case of the Negro is hopeless, the "educated" Negro decides upon the course of personally profiting by whatever he can do in using these people as a means to an end. He grins in their faces while "extracting money" from them, but his heart shows no fond attachment to their despised cause. With a little larger income than they receive he can make himself somewhat comfortable in the ghetto; and he forgets those who have no way of escape.

Some of this "educated" class join with unprincipled real estate men in keeping Negroes out of desirable parts of the city and confining them to unsanitary sections. Such persons help the profiteer to collect from Negroes thus cornered a larger rental than that exacted from whites for the same property. In similar fashion a Negro minister sometimes goes into a community where the races are moving along amicably together in their churches and rents a shack or an old empty store to start a separate church for "our people," not to supply any practical need but to exploit those who have never learned to think. Professional men, too, walking in their footsteps, impose also upon the poor innocent Negroes who do not know when they are being treated properly and when they are not, but high fees may be obtained from them inasmuch as they cannot always go to others for service.

Settling in a community with mixed schools,

105

the educated Negro often advocates their separation that his daughter may secure a position in the system. The Negro politician is accustomed to corner the Negro vote, by opening a separate office from which he may bargain with the chieftains of the machine for the highest price available. When paid off by some position, which is not very lofty, this officeholder accepts such employment with the understanding that he will be set off by himself as if he were destructive of the rest of mankind.

In the present crisis, however, the "highly educated" Negroes find very little to exploit, and in their untoward condition they have no program of finding a way out. They see numerous instances of Negroes losing their jobs in white establishments. In fact, these things occur daily. Janitors who have been giving satisfaction are abruptly told that they will no longer be needed. Negro waiters in hotels are being informed that their places will go to white workers. Negro truck drivers are ordered to step down and let the needy of the other race go up. We hear so much of this that we wonder what the outcome will be.

In this readjustment, of course, when there are fewer opportunities left for those who cannot or do not have the opportunity to operate machines the Negroes will naturally be turned out of their positions by their employers who think first of their own race. In the ultimate passing of the depression, however, Negroes will not be much better off when some of the whites now displacing them will rise to higher levels. In the economic order of tomorrow there will be little use for the factotum or scullion. Man will not need such personal attention when he can buy a machine to serve him more efficiently. The menial Negroes, the aggregate of parasites whom the "highly educated" Negro has exploited, will not be needed on tomorrow. What, then, will become of "our highly educated" Negroes who have no initiative?

We have appealed to the talented tenth for a remedy, but they have nothing to offer. Their minds have never functioned in this all-important sphere. The "educated" Negro shows no evidence of vision. He should see a new picture. The Negroes are facing the alternative of rising in the sphere of production to supply their proportion of the manufacturers and merchants or of going down to the graves of paupers. The Negro must now do for himself or die out as the world undergoes readjustment. If the whites are to continue for some time in doing drudgery to the exclusion of Negroes, the latter must find another way out. Nothing forces this upon one more dramatically than when he learns that white women in Montgomery, Alabama, are coming to the back door of Negro homes asking for their washing. If the whites have reached this extremity, and they must be taken care of first, what will be left for the Negroes?

At this moment, then, the Negroes must begin to do the very thing which they have been taught that they cannot do. They still have some money, and they have needs to supply. They must begin immediately to pool their earnings and organize industries to participate in supplying social and economic demands. If the Negroes are to remain forever removed from the producing atmosphere, and the present discrimination continues, there will be nothing left for them to do.

There is no reason for lack of confidence because of the recent failure of Negro enterprises, although the "highly educated" Negroes assert the contrary. This lack of confidence is the cause of the failure of these enterprises. If the Negroes had manifested enough confidence in them and had properly supported them, they would have been strong enough to stand the test in the crisis. Negro banks, as a rule, have failed because the people, taught that their own pioneers in business cannot function in this sphere, withdrew their deposits. An individual cannot live after you extract the blood from his veins. The strongest bank in the United States will last only so long as the people will have sufficient confidence in it to keep their money there. In fact, the confidence of the people is worth more than money.

The lack of confidence of the Negro in himself and in his possibilities is what has kept him down. His mis-education has been a perfect success in this respect. Yet it is not necessary for the Negro to have more confidence in his own workers than in others. If the Negro would be as fair to his own as he has been to others, this would be all that is necessary to give him a new lease on life and start the trend upward.

Here we find that the Negro has failed to recover from his slavish habit of berating his own and worshipping others as perfect beings. No progress has been made in this respect because the more "education" the Negro gets the worse off he is. He has just had so much longer to learn to decry and despise himself. The race looking to this educated class for a solution of its problems does not find any remedy; and, on the contrary, sees itself further and further away from those things to which it has aspired. By forgetting the schoolroom for the time being and relying upon an awakening of the masses through adult education we can do much to give the Negro a new point of view with respect to economic enterprise and group cooperation. The average Negro has not been sufficiently mis-educated to become hopeless.

Our minds must become sufficiently developed to use segregation to kill segregation, and thus bring to pass that ancient and yet modern prophecy, "The wrath of man shall praise thee." If the Negro in the ghetto must eternally be fed by the hand that pushes him into the ghetto, he will never become strong enough to get out of the ghetto. This assumption of Negro leadership in the ghetto, then, must not be confined to matters of religion, education, and social uplift; it must deal with such fundamental forces in life as make these things possible. If the Negro area, however, is to continue as a district supported wholly from without, the inept dwellers therein will merit and will receive only the contempt of those who may occasionally catch glimpses of them in their plight.

As Frederick Douglass said in 1852, "It is vain that we talk of being men, if we do not the work of men. We must become valuable to society in other departments of industry than those servile ones from which we are rapidly being excluded. We must show that we can do as well as they. When we can build as well as live in houses; when we can make as well as wear shoes; when we can produce as well as consume wheat, corn and rye—then we shall become valuable to society.

"Society," continued Douglass, "is a hard-hearted affair. With it the helpless may expect no higher dignity than that of paupers. The individual must lay society under obligation to him or society will honor him only as a stranger and sojourner."

110

CHAPTER XI

IN this untoward situation the Negro finds himself at the close of the third generation from Emancipation. He has been educated in the sense that persons directed a certain way are more easily controlled, or as Ovid remarked, "In time the bull is brought to bear the yoke." The Negro in this state continues as a child. He is restricted in his sphere to small things, and with these he becomes satisfied. His ambition does not rise any higher than to plunge into the competition with his fellows for these trifles. At the same time those who have given the race such false ideals are busy in the higher spheres from which Negroes by their mis-education and racial guidance have been disbarred.

Examples of this failure of the mis-educated Negro to have high ideals may be cited. The author has known numerous cases of Negro lawyers, physicians and business men who, while attending local Sunday schools, churches, and lodges, have fallen out about trifles like a resolution or the chairmanship of a committee, which so embittered them as to make themselves enemies for life and stumblingblocks preventing any such thing as organization or community cooperation.

It is a common occurrence to see a Negro well situated as a minister or teacher aspiring to a political appointment which temporarily pays little more than what he is receiving and offers no distinction except that of being earmarked as a Jim Crow job set aside for some Negro who has served well the purposes of the bosses as a wardheeler in a campaign. Negroes who have begun promising business enterprises sometimes abandon them temporarily for the same sort of empty honor. In this way they have been known to hamper their business by incurring the displeasure of ambitious politicians who might otherwise patronize them.

Negroes of this point of view have developed in that part of the country where it is thought that the most distinguished persons in the community are those who hold and exploit the local offices or those who are further honored with positions in the state and nation. While this may apply in the case of their oppressors the few positions allotted the Negroes are magnified beyond all reasonable bounds. This comes as a natural result, however, for the "education" of the Negro requires it. The ambitious mis-educated Negro in the struggle for the little things allotted by others prevents any achievement of the people in matters more constructive.

Potentially the colored people are strong although they are actually weak.

This much-ado-about-nothing renders impossible cooperation, the most essential thing in the development of a people. The ambitious of this class do more to keep the race in a state of turmoil and to prevent it from serious community effort than all the other elements combined. The one has a job that the other wants; or the one is a leader of a successful faction, and the other is struggling to supplant him. Everything in the community, then, must yield ground to this puerile contest.

In one city of a few thousand Negroes there is no chance for community cooperation because of the antagonism of the Methodist and Baptist preachers in charge of the two largest churches. The one is determined to dictate the appointment of the teaching corps and the social welfare workers; the other is persistently struggling to undo everything accomplished by his opponent. The one is up today, and the other in ascendency tomorrow. Several efforts have been made to start business enterprises there, but none has succeeded because one faction tears down what the other builds up.

In another city the cleavage is along political lines. Preachers are there, but a lawyer and a dentist plunging into politics have dispossessed the clergy of the stage. The leader of one faction is so bitterly opposed to the other that

113

he even warns strangers against going to the home of his adversary. To present a sane proposition to the community through one of these leaders means local warfare rather than an effort to work together for the common good. Consequently, although there are thousands of Negroes living together in one quarter they have no business enterprises of worth. The selfish struggle for personal aggrandizement, which has not yet brought either faction more than an appointment on the police force or a clerkship in one of the city offices, thus blocks the social and economic progress of thousands of unoffending people.

In another state the ambition of the highly educated Negro is restricted to becoming principals of the high schools. The neglected state school has not developed sufficiently to become attractive. The warring area, then, is in the cities. In one of them, where several Negroes own considerable wealth which, if pooled and properly used, would produce all but wonderful results, the petty strife has been most disastrous. Little thought is given to social uplift, and economic effort is crushed by factional wrangling. Before the author had been in one of the towns an hour a stalwart of one faction sounded him on becoming a candidate for the position held by the principal of the high school. A few minutes thereafter another approached him for advice as to how "to get him out."

114

The high cost of this childishness to the community can be estimated only by taking into consideration the fact that this strife is all but endless. If it were a matter that developed now and then only to be forgotten by people directing their attention thereafter to more important things, it would not do much harm; but this confusion continues for years. Sometimes it grips a community for a whole generation, vitiating the entire life of the people.

In spite of the meager rewards, however, the idea of leadership looms high in the Negro mind. It always develops thus among oppressed people. The oppressor must have some dealing with the despised group, and rather than have contact with individuals he approaches the masses through his own spokesman. The term itself connotes a backward condition. In its strides upward a race shuffles off its leaders because they originate outside of the group. They constitute a load that sinks the oppressed in the mire of trials and tribulations.

Leadership is usually superimposed for the purpose of "directing the course of the ostracized group along sane lines." This was accomplished during the days of slavery by restricting the assembly of Negroes to certain times and places and compelling them to meet in the presence of a stipulated number of the "wisest and discreetest men of the community." These supervisors of the conduct of Negroes would prevent them from learning the truth which might make them "unruly" or ambitious to become free.

After the Negroes became free the same end was reached by employing a Negro or some white man to spy upon and report behind closed doors on a plan to enslave the Negroes' minds. In case that actual employment as a spy seemed too bold, the person to be used as such an instrument took up some sort of enterprise which the oppressors of the race warmly supported to give him the desired influence in the community. This "racial racketeer" might be a politician, minister, teacher, director of a community center, or head of a "social uplift agency." As long as he did certain things and expressed the popular opinion on questions he lacked nothing, and those who followed him found their way apparently better paid as the years went by. His leadership, then, was recognized and the ultimate undoing of the Negroes in the community was assured.

Such leadership, too, has continued into our day and it goes from bad to worse. The very service which this racial toady renders hardens him to the extent that he loses his soul. He becomes equal to any task the oppressor may impose upon him, and at the same time he becomes artful enough to press his case convincingly before the thoughtless multitude. What is right is sacrificed because everything that is right is not expedient; and what is expedient soon becomes unnecessary.

Recently a citizen, observing how we have been thus betrayed, suggested that there be called a national meeting to take steps for a program of development of the race from within under "a new leadership." Such a movement can be made to mean something, and then it can degenerate into an assembly of abuse and vituperation followed by the usual whereas-therefore-be-it-resolved effort which has never meant anything in the awakening and the development of an oppressed people.

The Negroes, however, will not advance far if they continue to waste their energy abusing those who misdirect and exploit them. The exploiters of the race are not so much at fault as the race itself. If Negroes persist in permitting themselves to be handled in this fashion they will always find some one at hand to impose upon them. The matter is one which rests largely with the Negroes themselves. The race will free itself from exploiters just as soon as it decides to do so. No one else can accomplish this task for the race. It must plan and do for itself.

Checking up on what they do, Negroes often find themselves giving money and moral support to various persons and institutions which influence the course of the race in the wrong way. They do not often ask themselves whether

117

the support thus given will redound in the long run to the good of the people with whom they are identified. They do not inquire whether the assistance thus given offers temporary relief but eventually results in irreparable loss. So many Negroes often do themselves harm when they actually believe that they are doing good. Under their present teachers they cannot easily learn to do any better, for such training as we undergo does not open our eyes sufficiently for us to see far ahead of us.

If the Negro could abandon the idea of leadership and instead stimulate a larger number of the race to take up definite tasks and sacrifice their time and energy in doing these things efficiently the race might accomplish something. The race needs workers, not leaders. Such workers will solve the problems which race leaders talk about and raise money to enable them to talk more and more about. When you hear a man talking, then, always inquire as to what he is doing or what he has done for humanity. Oratory and resolutions do not avail much. If they did, the Negro race would be in a paradise on earth. It may be well to repeat here the saying that old men talk of what they have done, young men of what they are doing, and fools of what they expect to do. The Negro race has a rather large share of the last mentioned class.

If we can finally succeed in translating the

idea of leadership into that of service, we may soon find it possible to lift the Negro to a higher level. Under leadership we have come into the ghetto; by service within the ranks we may work our way out of it. Under leadership we have been constrained to do the biddings of others; by service we may work out a program in the light of our own circumstances. Under leadership we have become poverty-stricken; by service we may teach the masses how to earn a living honestly. Under leadership we have been made to despise our own possibilities and to develop into parasites; by service we may prove sufficient unto the task of self-development and contribute our part to modern culture.

CHAPTER XII

IF the highly educated Negroes have not learned better the simple lessons of life one cannot expect the laboring classes to conduct themselves differently. In the large number of cases the employers of Negroes in common labor, in which most of them are now engaged, assert that there is no hope for advancement of Negroes in their employ because Negroes will not work under foremen of their own color. In other words, the average Negro has not yet developed to the point that one is willing to take orders from another of his own race.

While it is true that such an answer is often given as a mere excuse for not placing Negroes in responsible positions when it can be done without any particular trouble, the investigation among Negroes themselves reveals numerous facts to prove that there is more truth than falsehood in this statement. Hundreds of employes of African blood frankly say that they will not work under a Negro. One is afraid that the other may prosper more than he does and be recognized accordingly.

Some of these instances are interesting. A

head of one of the Government departments, in which Negro women are employed to do unskilled labor, reports that he placed in charge of the group of these workers an intelligent colored woman who seemed to have all of the necessary qualifications which he had found in other women thus employed. Those working under her, however, refused to obey instructions, kept the place in turmoil and soon destroyed the morale of the whole force. As soon as he placed a white woman in charge, however, order was reestablished on the premises, and everything moved along smoothly.

Another employer conducting a wholesale business placed a Negro foreman in charge of others of his race to function as one of the important departments of the establishment. The Negroes working under him, who had formerly taken orders without question from the white foreman, soon undertook to take liberties with the promoted Negro and to ignore his orders. Knowing that the Negro foreman was well qualified, however, and being personally interested in him, the employer instead of doing what so many others under such circumstances had done, dismissed those who refused to cooperate and supplied the vacancies with others until an efficient working force could thus be obtained. Only a few employers, however, have had such patience and have manifested such interest in the advancement of the Negro. As

121

a rule they merely dispose of Negro foremen with the excuse that one Negro will not take orders from another.

This refusal of Negroes to take orders from one another is due largely to the fact that slaveholders taught their bondmen that they were as good as or better than any others and, therefore, should not be subjected to any member of their race. If they were to be subordinated to some one it should be to the white man of superior culture and social position. This keeps the whole race on a lower level, restricted to the atmosphere of trifles which do not concern their traducers. The greater things of life which can be attained only by wise leadership, then, they have no way to accomplish.

The strong have always used this as a means of dealing with the so-called weaker races of the world. The Caucasian arrays the one against the other so that they may never combine their forces and thus deprive their so-called superiors of control over them, which they could easily do if organized. One white man was thus able to maintain himself on a plantation where there were thirty or forty slaves because the Negroes were mis-educated in such a way as to keep them divided into distinct factions. In petty strife their power would be lost in the process of attrition. Today we find the same thing in Africa where this end is reached by embittering one tribe against another; and it worked the same way in India until recently when it began to break down under the masterful leadership of Mahatma Gandhi.

The Negroes of the United States have followed leadership slavishly but sometimes unfortunately that of those leaders who are selected for them by the traducers of the race. The enemies of the race, for example, will find a Negro willing to do certain things they desire to have accomplished and will finance him and give him sufficient publicity to get before the world, for the few favors which he may dispense among his followers as a result of his influence and economic position will bring to him the adequate number of Negroes for the constituency which he desires.

Negroes, however, sometimes choose their own leaders but unfortunately they are too often of the wrong kind. Negroes do not readily follow persons with constructive programs. Almost any sort of exciting appeal or trivial matter presented to them may receive immediate attention and temporarily at least liberal support. When the bubble collapses, of course, these same followers will begin to decry Negro leadership and call these misrepresentatives of the group rascals and scoundrels. Inasmuch as they have failed to exercise foresight, however, those who have deceived them should not be blamed so much as those who have liberally supported these impostors. Yet the fault here is not inherently in the Negro but in what he has been taught.

The Negroes' point of view, therefore, must be changed before they can construct a program which will bring them out of the wilderness. For example, no good can be expected from one of our teachers who said that she had to give up her class in Sunday school to accept an extra job of waiting on table at that hour because she had bought a twenty-four-hundred-dollar coat and her husband had purchased an expensive car. Such a teacher has no message for the Negro child. Her example would tend to drag the youth downward, and the very thought of having such a person in the schoolroom is most depressing.

We must feel equally discouraged when we see a minister driving up to his church on Sunday morning in a Cadillac. He does not come to feed the multitude spiritually. He comes to fleece the flock. The appeal he makes is usually emotional. While the people are feeling happy the expensive machine is granted, and the prolonged vacation to use it is easily financed. Thus the thoughtless drift backward toward slavery.

When you see a physician drive to one's door in his Pierce Arrow, you cannot get the impression he has come to treat the patient for a complaint. He has come to treat him for a dollar. Such physicians, as a rule, know less and less medicine as the years go by, although they make much money by learning human psychology and using it for personal gain. With leeches of this type feeding upon an all but impoverished people and giving them nothing back there can be no hope for advancement.

No people can go forward when the majority of those who should know better have chosen to go backward, but this is exactly what most of our misleaders do. Not being learned in the history and background of the race, they figure out that there is no hope for the masses; and they decide, then, that the best thing they can do is to exploit these people for all they can and use the accumulations selfishly. Such persons have no vision and therefore perish at their own hands.

It is an injustice to the Negro, however, to mis-educate him and suffer his manners to be corrupted from infancy unto old age and then blame him for making the mistakes which such guidance necessitates. "People who have been restricted and held down naturally condescend to the lower levels of delinquency. When education has been entirely neglected or improperly managed we see the worst passions ruling with uncontrolled and incessant sway. Good sense degenerates into craft, anger wrangles into malignity, restraint which is thought most solitary comes too late, and the most judicial admonitions are urged in vain."

125

Philosophers have long conceded, however, that every man has two educations: "that which is given to him, and the other that which he gives himself. Of the two kinds the latter is by far the more desirable. Indeed all that is most worthy in man he must work out and conquer for himself. It is that which constitutes our real and best nourishment. What we are merely taught seldom nourishes the mind like that which we teach ourselves."

The same eternal principle applies to a race forced to live apart from others as a separate and distinct group. Inasmuch as the education of the Negro has come from without we can clearly see that he has received only a part of the development which he should have undergone or he has developed negatively. The Negro lacks mental power, which cannot be expected from ill-fed brains.

This naturally brings up a serious question. The people on the outside, who are directing the race from afar, will take this condition of affairs as evidence that the Negro is not prepared for leadership. What they ought to say is that they have not prepared the Negro to assume the responsibility of his own uplift. Instead of doing this, however, they play up this result of their own failure as an argument for imposing upon the Negro race the guidance of others from without.

As to whether or not a white man should be a

leader of the Negroes may be dismissed as a silly question. What has the color to do with it? Such a worker may be white, brown, yellow, or red, if he is heart and soul with the people whom he would serve. It just happens, however, that most white men now in control of Negro institutions are not of this required type. Practically all of those with whom I have talked and communicated believe in imposing some sort of disability upon Negroes. Some object to the freedom of intermarriage as a substitute for concubinage, scoff at the idea of the enfranchisement of the Negroes, approve their segregation, and justify the economic exploitation of the race. Now if these are the persons to elevate the Negroes, to what point do they expect to lift them, and what will the Negroes be when they get there?

With this same thought in mind a white director of Negroes recently said to the author:

"I realize that I have no useful function in my present position as a president of a Negro institution. I do not approve of their aspirations to many things. I cannot accept the students in my house as I would white students because it might lead to an interracial romance. Marrying is such a difficult problem at the best that I should not like to see one of my children make a failure in life by marrying a Negro."

"In other words," continued he, "we live in two different worlds. While I am among them

I cannot become a part of them. How then can I help them under these circumstances?''

I am acquainted with another white educator at the head of a Negro institution, who will not address a colored girl as Miss, and to avoid the use of a title in speaking to women of the race he addresses them as his kin. One of them was sharp enough to reply to him thus when he accosted her as auntie:

''Oh, I am so glad that I have found my lost relatives at last. My mother often told me that I had some distinguished kin, and just to think that you are my nephew makes me feel glad.''

Another such exploiter in charge of a Negro college never wears his hat on the campus. His confidential explanation is that he might have to lift it when he meets a Negro woman. Of course, that would never do. ''White supremacy'' would be lost in the Negro school.

As we realize more and more that education is not merely imparting information which is expected to produce certain results, we see very clearly the inconsistency of the position of white persons as executives of Negro institutions. These misfits belong to the very group working out the segregation of the Negro, and they come into these institutions mainly to earn a living. They make no particular contribution to the development of education, for they are not scholarly enough to influence educational theory; and they are so far out of sympathy with the Negro that they cannot make any contribution to educational practice. These "foreigners" are not bringing to such institutions large sums of money which the Negroes cannot obtain, for the institutions now directed by Negroes are receiving larger appropriations than those under the management of whites.

Our so-called thinkers, however, seldom see the inevitable results of this unsound policy. Not long ago when the author wrote the textbook entitled NEGRO MAKERS OF HISTORY it was adversely criticised by a Negro who said that the book should have had as an illustration the cut of the white man who established a certain Negro college. The author had to explain that the book was to give an account of what the Negro has done, not of what has been done for him.

The school referred to, moreover, was in no sense a Negro school. It had very few Negro teachers and only one Negro trustee. The policy of the school was determined altogether by others without giving the Negro credit for having a thought on education. In other words, it was merely a school which Negroes were permitted to attend. If they picked up here and there something to help them, well and good; if not, may God help them!

It is all right to have a white man as the head of a Negro college or to have a red man at the head of a yellow one, if in each case the incumbent has taken out his naturalization papers and has identified himself as one of the group which he is trying to serve. It seems that the white educators of this day are unwilling to do this, and for that reason they can never contribute to the actual development of the Negro from within. You cannot serve people by giving them orders as to what to do. The real servant of the people must live among them, think with them, feel for them, and die for them.

The white worker in Negro institutions, too, can never be successful without manifesting some faith in the people with whom he has cast his lot. His efforts must not be merely an attempt to stimulate their imitation of things in a foreign sphere. He must study his community sufficiently to discover the things which have a trend in the proper direction that he may stimulate such forces and thus help the community to do better the good things which it may be capable of doing and at the same time may be interested in doing. If these people are to be brought the ideas of "foreigners," and must be miraculously transformed into something else before anything can be made of them, such effort will be a fruitless task like most of the so-called education and uplift of the Negroes in America.

The Negro, in spite of his confinement to the ghetto, has some opportunities to develop his special capacities if they are properly studied and understood. The real servant of the people, then, will give more attention to those to be served than to the use that somebody may want to make of them. He will be more concerned with what he can do to increase the ease, comfort, and happiness of the Negro than with how the Negro may be used to contribute to the ease, comfort, and happiness of others.

The servant of the people, unlike the leader, is not on a high horse elevated above the people and trying to carry them to some designated point to which he would like to go for his own advantage. The servant of the people is down among them, living as they live, doing what they do and enjoying what they enjoy. He may be a little better informed than some other members of the group; it may be that he has had some experience that they have not had, but in spite of this advantage he should have more humility than those whom he serves, for we are told that "Whosoever is greatest among you, let him be your servant."

CHAPTER XIII

UNDERSTAND THE NEGRO

"We do not offer here any course in Negro history, Negro literature, or race relations," recently said a professor of a Negro college. "We study the Negro along with other people."

"An excellent idea," the interviewer replied. "No one should expect you to do any more than this, but how do you do it when the Negro is not mentioned in your textbooks except to be condemned? Do you, a teacher in a Negro school, also condemn the race in the same fashion as the writers of your textbooks of history and literature?"

"No," said he, "we bring the Negro in here and there."

"How often does 'here and there' connote?"

"Well, you know," said he, "Negroes have not done much; and what they have accomplished may be briefly covered by referring to the achievements of a few men and women.

"Why do you emphasize the special study of the Negro?" said he further. "Why is it necessary to give the race special attention in the press, on the rostrum, or in the schoolroom? This idea of projecting the Negro into the foreground does the race much harm by singing continually of his woes and problems and thus alienating the public which desires to give its attention to other things.''

It is true that many Negroes do not desire to hear anything about their race, and few whites of today will listen to the story of woe. With most of them the race question has been settled. The Negro has been assigned to the lowest drudgery as the sphere in which the masses must toil to make a living; and socially and politically the race has been generally proscribed. Inasmuch as the traducers of the race have ''settled'' the matter in this fashion, they naturally oppose any effort to change this status.

Many Negro professional men who are making a living attending to the affairs of these laborers and servants in their mentally undeveloped state and many teachers who in conservative fashion are instructing their children to maintain the *status quo ante bellum,* also oppose any movement to upset this arrangement. They are getting paid for their efforts. Why should they try innovations? The gods have so decreed it. Human beings cannot change it. Why be foolish?

A Negro with sufficient thought to construct a program of his own is undesirable, and the educational systems of this country generally refuse to work through such Negroes in promoting their cause. The program for the uplift of the Negroes in this country must be handed over to an executive force like orders from the throne, and they must carry it out without question or get out of line and let the procession go on. Although the Negro is being daily forced more and more by segregation into a world peculiarly his own, his unusually perplexing status is given little or no thought, and he is not considered capable of thinking for himself.

The chief difficulty with the education of the Negro is that it has been largely imitation resulting in the enslavement of his mind. Somebody outside of the race has desired to try out on Negroes some experiment which interested him and his coworkers; and Negroes, being objects of charity, have received them cordially and have done what they required. In fact, the keynote in the education of the Negro has been to do what he is told to do. Any Negro who has learned to do this is well prepared to function in the American social order as others would have him.

Looking over the courses of study of the public schools, one finds little to show that the Negro figures in these curricula. In supplementary matter a good deed of some Negro is occasionally referred to, but oftener the race is mentioned only to be held up to ridicule. With the exception of a few places like Atlantic City, Atlanta, Tulsa, St. Louis, Birmingham, Knox-

ville, and the states of Louisiana and North
Carolina no effort is made to study the Negro
in the public schools as they do the Latin, the
Teuton, or the Mongolian. Several mis-educated
Negroes themselves contend that the study of
the Negro by children would bring before them
the race problem prematurely and, therefore,
urge that the study of the race be deferred until
they reach advanced work in the college or university. These misguided teachers ignore the
fact that the race question is being brought before black and white children daily in their
homes, in the streets, through the press and on
the rostrum. How, then, can the school ignore
the duty of teaching the truth while these other
agencies are playing up falsehood?

The experience of college instructors shows
that racial attitudes of the youth are not easily
changed after they reach adolescence. Although
students of this advanced stage are shown the
fallacy of race superiority and the folly of social
distinctions, they nevertheless continue to do
the illogical thing of still looking upon these
depised groups as less worthy than themselves and persist in treating them accordingly.
Teachers of elementary and secondary schools
giving attention to this interracial problem have
succeeded in softening and changing the attitude of children whose judgment has not been
so hopelessly warped by the general attitude

of the communities in which they have been brought up.

In approaching this problem in this fashion to counteract the one-sided education of youth the thinking people of this country have no desire to upset the curricula of the schools or to force the Negro as such into public discussion; but, if the Negro is to be elevated he must be educated in the sense of being developed from what he is, and the public must be so enlightened as to think of the Negro as a man. Furthermore, no one can be thoroughly educated until he learns as much about the Negro as he knows about other people.

Upon examining the recent catalogues of the leading Negro colleges, one finds that invariably they give courses in ancient, mediæval, and modern Europe, but they do not give such courses in ancient, mediæval, and modern Africa. Yet Africa, according to recent discoveries, has contributed about as much to the progress of mankind as Europe has, and the early civilization of the Mediterranean world was decidedly influenced by Africa.

Negro colleges offer courses bearing on the European colonists prior to their coming to America, their settlement on these shores, and their development here toward independence. Why are they not equally generous with the Negroes in treating their status in Africa prior to enslavement, their first transplantation to

the West Indies, the Latinization of certain
Negroes in contradistinction to the development of others under the influence of the
Teuton, and the effort of the race toward self-
expression?

A further examination of their curricula
shows, too, that invariably these Negro colleges
offer courses in Greek philosophy and in that of
modern European thought, but they direct no
attention to the philosophy of the African.
Negroes of Africa have and always have had
their own ideas about the nature of the universe,
time, and space, about appearance and reality,
and about freedom and necessity. The effort of
the Negro to interpret man's relation to the
universe shows just as much intelligence as we
f nd in the philosophy of the Greeks. There
were many Africans who were just as wise as
Socrates.

Again, one observes in some of these catalogues numerous courses in art but no well de-
fined course in Negro or African art which
early influenced that of the Greeks. Thinkers
are now saying that the early culture of the
Mediterranean was chiefly African. Most of
these colleges do not even direct special attention to Negro music in which the Negro has
made his outstanding contribution in America.
The unreasonable attitude is that because the
whites do not have these things in their schools
the Negroes must not have them in theirs. The

Catholics and Jews, therefore, are wrong in establishing special schools to teach their principles of religion, and the Germans in America are unwise in having their children taught their mother tongue.

Such has been the education of Negroes. They have been taught facts of history, but have never learned to think. Their conception is that you go to school to find out what other people have done, and then you go out in life to imitate them. What they have done can be done by others, they contend; and they are right. They are wrong, however, in failing to realize that what others have done, we may not need to do. If we are to do identically the same thing from generation to generation, we would not make any progress. If we are to duplicate from century to century the same feats, the world will grow tired of such a monotonous performance.

In this particular respect "Negro education" is a failure, and disastrously so, because in its present predicament the race is especially in need of vision and invention to give humanity something new. The world does not want and will never have the heroes and heroines of the past. What this age needs is an enlightened youth not to undertake the tasks like theirs but to imbibe the spirit of these great men and answer the present call of duty with equal nobleness of soul.

Not only do the needs of generations vary, but the individuals themselves are not duplicates the one of the other; and being different in this respect, their only hope to function efficiently in society is to know themselves and the generation which they are to serve. The chief value in studying the records of others is to become better acquainted with oneself and with one's possibilities to live and to do in the present age. As long as Negroes continue to restrict themselves to doing what was necessary a hundred or a thousand years ago, they must naturally expect to be left out of the great scheme of things as they concern men of today.

The most inviting field for discovery and invention, then, is the Negro himself, but he does not realize it. Frederika Bremer, when reflecting upon her visit to America about 1850, gave this country a new thought in saying to Americans, "The romance of your history is the fate of the Negro." In this very thought lies unusual possibilities for the historian, the economist, the artist, and the philosopher. Why should the Negro writer seek a theme abroad when he has the greatest of all at home?

The bondage of the Negro brought captive from Africa is one of the greatest dramas in history, and the writer who merely sees in that ordeal something to approve or condemn fails to understand the evolution of the human race. Negroes now studying dramatics go into our schools to reproduce Shakespeare, but mentally developed members of this race would see the possibilities of a greater drama in the tragedy of the man of color. Negroes graduating from conservatories of music dislike the singing of our folk songs. For some reason such misguided persons think that they can improve on the productions of the foreign drama or render the music of other people better than they can themselves.

A knowledge of real history would lead one to think that slavery was one of the significant developments which, although evil in themselves, may redound sometimes to the advantage of the oppressed rather than to that of the oppressor. Some one has said that the music of Poland was inspired by incidents of a struggle against the despots invading and partitioning their prostrate land. The Greeks never had an art until the country was overrun by hostile Orientals. Some one then began to immortalize in song the sons who went forth to fight for the native land. Another carved in marble the thought evoked by the example of the Greek youth who blocked the mountain pass with his body or who bared his breast to the javelin to defend the liberty of his country. These things we call art.

In our own country the other elements of the population, being secure in their position, have never faced such a crisis; and the Europeans, after whose pattern American life is fashioned, have not recently had such experience. White Americans, then, have produced no art at all, and that of Europe has reached the point of stagnation. Negroes who are imitating whites, then, are engaged in a most unprofitable performance. Why not interpret themselves anew to the world?

If we had a few thinkers we could expect great achievements on tomorrow. Some Negro with unusual insight would write an epic of bondage and freedom which would take its place with those of Homer and Virgil. Some Negro with esthetic appreciation would construct from collected fragments of Negro music a grand opera that would move humanity to repentance. Some Negro of philosophic penetration would find a solace for the modern world in the soul of the Negro, and then men would be men because they are men.

The Negro in his present plight, however, does not see possibilities until it is too late. He exercises much "hindsight," and for that reason he loses ground in the hotly contested battles of life. The Negro as a rule waits until a thing happens before he tries to avert it. He is too much like a man whom the author once saw knocked down in a physical combat. Instead of dodging the blow when it was being dealt he arose from his prostration dodging it.

For example, the author has just received a

141

letter from a lady in Pittsburgh complaining that the librarian in one of its schools insists upon reading to the children "a great deal of literature containing such words as 'nigger,' 'Blackie,' 'Little Black Sambo,' etc." This lady, therefore, would like to place in that school some books by Negro authors. This is a commendable effort, but it comes a little late; we hope not too late.

For centuries such literature has been circulated among the children of the modern world; and they have, therefore, come to regard the Negro as inferior. Now that some of our similarly mis-educated Negroes are seeing how they have been deceived they are awakening to address themselves to a long neglected work. They should have been thinking about this generations ago, for they have a tremendous task before them today in dispelling this error and counteracting the results of such bias in our literature.

There has just come, too, from a friend of humanity in Edinburgh, Scotland, a direful account of the increase in race prejudice in those parts. Sailors who had frequented the stronghold of race prejudice in South Africa undertook recently to prevent Negro men from socializing with Scotch women at a dance; and certain professors of the University of Edinburgh with the same attitude show so much of it in their teaching that this friend entreats us to send them informing books on the Negro. We are doing it.

Here again, however, the effort to uproot error and popularize the truth comes rather late. The Negro since freedom has gone along grinning, whooping, and "cutting capers" while the white man has applied himself to the task of defining the status of the Negro and compelling him to accept it as thus settled forever. While the Negro has been idle, propaganda has gone far ahead of history. Unfortunately, too, Negro "scholars" have assisted in the production of literature which gives this point of view.

CHAPTER XIV

THE NEW PROGRAM

It seems only a reasonable proposition, then, that, if under the present system which produced our leadership in religion, politics, and business we have gone backward toward serfdom or have at least been kept from advancing to real freedom, it is high time to develop another sort of leadership with a different educational system. In the first place, we must bear in mind that the Negro has never been educated. He has merely been informed about other things which he has not been permitted to do. The Negroes have been shoved out of the regular schools through the rear door into the obscurity of the backyard and told to imitate others whom they see from afar, or they have been permitted in some places to come into the public schools to see how others educate themselves. The program for the uplift of the Negro in this country must be based upon a scientific study of the Negro from within to develop in him the power to do for himself what his oppressors will never do to elevate him to the level of others.

Being without actual education, we have very

few persons prepared to help the Negroes whom they have set out to lead. These persons are not all dishonest men and women. Many of them are sincere, and believe that they are doing the race some great good in thus holding it backward. They must be awakened and shown the error of their ways.

We have very few teachers because most of those with whom we are afflicted know nothing about the children whom they teach or about their parents who influence the pupils more than the teachers themselves. When a boy comes to school without knowing his lesson he should be studied instead of being punished. The boy who does well in the beginning of the year and lags behind near the end of the term should not always be censured or ridiculed. As a rule, such children are not responsible for their failures. Their parents and their social status account mainly for these shortcomings. The Negro teacher, then, must treat the disease rather than its symptoms.

But can you expect teachers to revolutionize the social order for the good of the community? Indeed we must expect this very thing. The educational system of a country is worthless unless it accomplishes this task. Men of scholarship and consequently of prophetic insight must show us the right way and lead us into the light which shines brighter and brighter.

In the church where we have much freedom

and independence we must get rid of preachers who are not prepared to help the people whom they exploit. The public must refuse to support men of this type. Ministers who are the creations of the old educational system must be awakened, and if this is impossible they must be dethroned. Those who keep the people in ignorance and play upon their emotions must be exiled. The people have never been taught what religion is, for most of the preachers find it easier to stimulate the superstition which develops in the unenlightened mind. Religion in such hands, then, becomes something with which you take advantage of weak people. Why try to enlighten the people in such matters when superstition serves just as well for exploitation?

The ministers with the confidence of the people must above all things understand the people themselves. They must find out the past of their parishioners, whether they were brought up in Georgia, Alabama or Texas, whether they are housed under desirable circumstances, what they do to make a living, what they do with their earnings, how they react to the world about them, how they spend their leisure, or how they function along with other elements of the social order.

In our schools, and especially in schools of religion, attention should be given to the study of the Negro as he developed during the antebellum period by showing to what extent that remote culture was determined by ideas which the Negro brought with him from Africa. To take it for granted that the ante-bellum Negro was an ignoramus or that the native brought from Africa had not a valuable culture merely because some prejudiced writers have said so does not show the attitude of scholarship, and Negro students who direct their courses accordingly will never be able to grapple with the social problems presented today by the Negro church.

The preachers of today must learn to do as well as those of old. Richard Allen so interpreted Christianity anew to his master that he was converted, and so did Henry Evans and George Bentley for other whites in North Carolina and Tennessee. Instead of accepting and trying to carry out the theories which the exploiters of humanity have brought them for a religious program the Negroes should forget their differences and in the strength of a united church bring out a new interpretation of Christ to this unwilling world. Following the religious teachings of their traducers, the Negroes do not show any more common sense than a people would in permitting criminals to enact the laws and establish the procedure of the courts by which they are to be tried.

Negro preachers, too, must be educated to their people rather than away from them. This, of course, requires a new type of religious school. To provide for such training the Negro church must get rid of its burdensome supervisory force. If the number of bishops of the various Negro Methodist churches were reduced to about twelve or fifteen, as they should be, the amount of a hundred thousand dollars or more now being paid to support the unnecessary number could be used to maintain properly at least one accredited college; and what is now being raised here and there to support various struggling but starving institutions kept alive by ambitious bishops and preachers could be saved to the people. With this money diverted to a more practical use the race would be able to establish some other things which would serve as assets rather than as liabilities.

We say liabilities, for practically all of our denominational schools which are bleeding the people for the inadequate support which they receive are still unable to do accredited work. There are so many of them that the one impoverishes the other. Outstanding men of the church, therefore, have to acquire their advanced education by attending other schools in the beginning or by taking additional training elsewhere after learning all our denominational schools can offer. This is a loss of ground which should be regained if the church is to go forward.

By proper unification and organization the Negro churches might support one or two much needed universities of their own. With the present arrangement of two or three in the same area and sometimes as many in one city there is no chance for emerging from the trying poverty-stricken state. And even if these institutions could do well what they undertake they do not supply all educational needs. To qualify for certification in the professions Negroes must go to other schools, where, although they acquire the fundamentals, they learn much about their "inferiority" to discourage them in their struggle upward.

We should not close any accredited Negro colleges or universities, but we should reconstruct the whole system. We should not eliminate many of the courses now being offered, but we should secure men of vision to give them from the point of view of the people to be served. We should not spend less money for the higher education of the Negro, but should redefine higher education as preparation to think and work out a program to serve the lowly rather than to live as an aristocrat.

Such subjects of certitude as mathematics, of course, would continue and so would most of the work in practical languages and science. In theology, literature, social science, and education, however, radical reconstruction is necessary. The old worn-out theories as to man's relation to God and his fellowman, the system of thought which has permitted one man to ex-

149

ploit, oppress, and exterminate another and still be regarded as righteous must be discarded for the new thought of men as brethren and the idea of God as the lover of all mankind.

After Negro students have mastered the fundamentals of English, the principles of composition, and the leading facts in the development of its literature, they should not spend all of their time in advanced work on Shakespeare, Chaucer and Anglo-Saxon. They should direct their attention also to the folklore of the African, to the philosophy in his proverbs, to the development of the Negro in the use of modern language, and to the works of Negro writers.

The leading facts of the history of the world should be studied by all, but of what advantage is it to the Negro student of history to devote all of his time to courses bearing on such despots as Alexander the Great, Cæsar, and Napoleon, or to the record of those nations whose outstanding achievement has been rapine, plunder, and murder for world power? Why not study the African background from the point of view of anthropology and history, and then take up sociology as it concerns the Negro peasant or proletarian who is suffering from sufficient ills to supply laboratory work for the most advanced students of the social order? Why not take up economics as reflected by the Negroes of today and work out some remedy for their lack of capital, the absence of cooperative enterprise, and the short life of their establishments. Institutions like Harvard, Yale and Columbia are not going to do these things, and educators influenced by them to the extent that they become blind to the Negro will never serve the race efficiently.

To educate the Negro we must find out exactly what his background is, what he is today, what his possibilities are, and how to begin with him as he is and make him a better individual of the kind that he is. Instead of cramming the Negro's mind with what others have shown that they can do, we should develop his latent powers that he may perform in society a part of which others are not capable.

During his life the author has seen striking examples of how people should and should not be taught. Some of these are worth relating. Probably the most interesting was that of missionary work in China. In 1903 the author crossed the Pacific Ocean with twenty-six missionaries who were going to take the Orient by storm. One Todd, from North Carolina, was orating and preaching almost every day to stimulate his coworkers to go boldly to the task before them. Dr. De Forest, long a missionary to Japan, informed them that the work required more than enthusiasm; that they could not rush into the homes of the natives saying, "Peace be to this house," for it might turn out the other way and give somebody the opportunity to say, "Peace be to his ashes."

Dr. De Forest explained to them how he chose a decidedly different course, preferring first to study the history, the language, the manners and the customs of the people to approach them intelligently; and not until he had been in the country four years did he undertake to exhort, but after that time he had had great success and had been invited to preach before the Mikado himself. Now Todd did not take this advice, and he had not been in China five months before he and his wife had been poisoned by their native cook who had become incensed at the way they interfered with the institutions of his people.

Another striking illustration was the education of the Filipinos. Not long after the close of the Spanish-American War the United States Government started out to educate the Filipinos over night. Numbers of "highly trained" Americans were carried there to do the work. They entered upon their task by teaching the Filipinos just as they had taught American children who were otherwise circumstanced. The result was failure. Men trained at institutions like Harvard, Yale, Columbia, and Chicago could not reach these people and had to be dismissed from the service. Some of these "scholarly" Americans had to be maintained by the subscription of friends until they could be returned to this country on Government transportation.

In the meantime, however, there came along an insurance man, who went to the Philippines to engage in business. He had never taught at all, and he had never studied authorities like Bagley, Judd, and Thorndike; but he understood people. Seeing that others had failed, he went into the work himself. He filled the schoolroom with thousands of objects from the pupil's environment. In the beginning he did not use books very much, because those supplied were not adapted to the needs of the children. He talked about the objects around them. Everything was presented objectively. When he took up the habits of the snake he brought the reptile to the school for demonstration. When he taught the crocodile he had one there. In teaching the Filipinos music he did not sing "Come shake the Apple-Tree." They had never seen such an object. He taught them to sing "Come shake the Lomboy Tree," something which they had actually done. In reading he did not concentrate on the story of how George Washington always told the truth. They had never heard of him and could not have appreciated that myth if some one had told them about it. This real educator taught them about their own hero, José Rizal, who gave his life as a martyr for the freedom of his country. By and by they got rid of most books based on the life of

153

American people and worked out an entirely
new series dealing with the life of Filipinos.
The result, then, was that this man and others
who saw the situation as he did succeeded, and
the work of the public schools in the Philippines
is today the outstanding achievement of the
Americans in that country.

We do not mean to suggest here, however,
that any people should ignore the record of
the progress of other races. We would not
advocate any such unwise course. We say,
hold on to the real facts of history as they are,
but complete such knowledge by studying also
the history of races and nations which have been
purposely ignored. We should not underrate
the achievements of Mesopotamia, Greece, and
Rome; but we should give equally as much attention to the internal African kingdoms, the
Songhay empire, and Ethiopia, which through
Egypt decidedly influenced the civilization of
the Mediterranean world. We would not ignore
the rise of Christianity and the development
of the Church; but we would at the same
time give honorable mention to the persons of
African blood who figured in these achievements, and who today are endeavoring to carry
out the principles of Jesus long since repudiated
by most so-called Christians. We would not
underestimate the achievements of the captains
of industry who in the commercial expansion of
the modern world have produced the wealth

154

necesary to ease and comfort; but we would give credit to the Negro who so largely supplied the demand for labor by which these things have been accomplished.

In our own particular history we would not dim one bit the lustre of any star in our firmament. We would not learn less of George Washington, "First in War, First in Peace and First in the Hearts of his Countrymen"; but we would learn something also of the three thousand Negro soldiers of the American Revolution who helped to make this "Father of our Country" possible. We would not neglect to appreciate the unusual contribution of Thomas Jefferson to freedom and democracy; but we would invite attention also to two of his outstanding contemporaries, Phillis Wheatley, the writer of interesting verse, and Benjamin Banneker, the mathematician, astronomer, and advocate of a world peace plan set forth in 1793 with the vital principles of Woodrow Wilson's League of Nations. We would in no way detract from the fame of Perry on Lake Erie or Jackson at New Orleans in the second struggle with England; but we would remember the gallant black men who assisted in winning these memorable victories on land and sea. We would not cease to pay tribute to Abraham Lincoln as the "Savior of the Country"; but we would ascribe praise also to the one hundred and seventy-eight thousand Negroes who had to be mustered into the service of the Union before it could be preserved, and who by their heroism demonstrated that they were entitled to freedom and citizenship.

CHAPTER XV

BUT how can the Negro in this new system learn to make a living, the most important task to which all people must give attention? In view of the Negro's economic plight most of the schools are now worked up over what is called "vocational guidance" in an effort to answer this very question. To what, however, are they to guide their Negro students? Most Negroes now employed are going down blind alleys, and unfortunately some schools seem to do no more than to stimulate their going in that direction.

This may seem to be a rash statement, but a study of our educational system shows that our schools are daily teaching Negroes what they can never apply in life or what is no longer profitable because of the revolution of industry by the multiplication of mechanical appliances. For example, some of our schools are still teaching individual garment making which offers no future today except in catering to the privileged and rich classes. Some of these institutions still offer instruction in shoemaking when the technique developed under their handicaps makes impossible competition with that of the modern factory based upon the invention of a Negro, Jan Matzeliger.

These facts have been known for generations, but some of these institutions apparently change not. Education, like religion, is conservative. It makes haste slowly only, and sometimes not at all. Do not change the present order of thinking and doing, many say, for you disturb too many things long since regarded as ideal. The dead past, according to this view, must be the main factor in determining the future. We should learn from the living past, but let the dead past remain dead.

A survey of employment of the Negroes in this country shows a most undesirable situation. The education of the masses has not enabled them to advance very far in making a living and has not developed in the Negro the power to change this condition. It is revealed that in many establishments the Negro when a young man starts as a janitor or porter and dies in old age in the same position. Tradition fixes his status as such, and both races feel satisfied.

When this janitor or porter dies the dailies headline the passing of this Negro who knew his place and rendered satisfactory service in it. "Distinguished" white men, for whom he ran errands and cleaned cuspidors, volunteer as honorary pall-bearers and follow his remains to the final resting place. Thoughtless Negro editors, instead of expressing their regret that such a life of usefulness was not rewarded by promotion, take up the refrain as some great honor bestowed upon the race.

Among people thus satisfied in the lower pursuits of life and sending their children to school to memorize theories which they never see applied, there can be no such thing as vocational guidance. Such an effort implies an objective; and in the present plight of economic dependence there is no occupation for which the Negro may prepare himself with the assurance that he will find employment. Opportunities which he has today may be taken from him tomorrow; and schools changing their curricula in hit-and-miss fashion may soon find themselves on the wrong track just as they have been for generations.

Negroes do not need some one to guide them to what persons of another race have developed. They must be taught to think and develop something for themselves. It is most pathetic to see Negroes begging others for a chance as we have been doing recently. "Do not force us into starvation," we said. "Let us come into your stores and factories and do a part of what you are doing to profit by our trade." The Negro as a slave developed this fatal sort of dependency; and, restricted mainly to menial service and drudgery during nominal freedom, he has not grown out of it. Now the Negro is facing the ordeal of either learning to do for himself or to die out gradually in the bread line in the ghetto.

If the schools really mean to take a part in necessary uplift they must first supply themselves with teachers. Unfortunately we have very few such workers. The large majority of persons supposedly teaching Negroes never carry to the schoolroom any thought as to improving their condition. From the point of view of these so-called teachers they have done their duty when in automaton fashion they impart in the schoolroom the particular facts which they wrote out in the examination when they "qualified" for their respective positions. Most of them are satisfied with receiving their pay and spending it for the toys and gewgaws of life.

For example, the author is well acquainted with a Negro of this type, who is now serving as the head of one of the largest schools in the United States. From the point of view of our present system he is well educated. He holds advanced degrees from one of the leading institutions of the world; and he is known to be well informed on all the educational theories developed from the time of Socrates down to the day of Dewey. Yet this "educator" says repeatedly that in his daily operations he never has anything to do with Negroes because they are impossible. He says that he never buys anything from a Negro store, and he would not dare to put a penny in a Negro bank.

From such teachers large numbers of Negroes learn this fateful lesson. For example, not long ago a committee of Negroes in a large city went to the owner of a chain store in their neighborhood and requested that he put a Negro manager in charge. This man replied that he doubted that the Negroes themselves wanted such a thing. The Negroes urging him to make the change assured him that they were unanimously in favor of it. The manager, however, asked them to be fair enough with his firm and themselves to investigate before pressing the matter any further. They did so and discovered that one hundred thirty-seven Negro families in that neighborhood seriously objected to buying from Negroes and using articles handled by them. These Negroes, then, had to do the groundwork of uprooting the inferiority idea which had resulted from their mis-education.

To what, then, can a Negro while despising the enterprise of his fellows guide the youth of his race; and where do you figure out that the youth thus guided will be by 1950? The whites are daily informing Negroes that they need not come to them for opportunities. Can the Negro youth, mis-educated by persons who depreciate their efforts, learn to make opportunities for themselves? This is the real problem which the Negroes must solve; and he who is not interested in it and makes no effort to solve it is worthless in the present struggle.

Our advanced teachers, like "most highly educated" Negroes, pay little attention to the things about them except when the shoe begins to pinch on one or the other side. Unless they happen to become naked they never think of the production of cotton or wool; unless they get hungry they never give any thought to the output of wheat or corn; unless their friends lose their jobs they never inquire about the outlook for coal or steel, or how these things affect the children whom they are trying to teach. In other words, they live in a world, but they are not of it. How can such persons guide the youth without knowing how these things affect the Negro community?

The Negro community, in a sense, is composed of those around you, but it functions in a different way. You cannot see it by merely looking out of the windows of the schoolroom. This community requires scientific investigation. While persons of African blood are compelled to sustain closer relation to their own people than to other elements in society, they are otherwise influenced socially and economically. The Negro community suffers for lack of delimitation because of the various ramifications of life in the United States. For example, there may be a Negro grocer in the neighborhood, but the Negro chauffeur for a rich man down town and the washerwoman for an aristocratic family in "quality row" will be more than apt to buy their food and clothing at the larger establishment with which their employers have connections, although they may be insulted there. Negroes of the District of Columbia have millions of dollars deposited in banks down town, where Negro women are not allowed in the ladies' rest rooms.

Right in the heart of the highly educated Negro section of Washington, too, is a restaurant catering through the front door exclusively to the white business men, who must live in the Negroes' section to supply them with the necessities of life, and catering at the same time through the back door to numbers of Negroes who pile into that dingy room to purchase whatever may be thrown at them. Yet less than two blocks away are several Negroes running cafés where they can be served for the same amount and under desirable circumstances. Negroes who do this, we say, do not have the proper attitude toward life and its problems, and for that reason we do not take up time with them. They do not belong to our community. The traducers of the race, however, are guiding these people the wrong way. Why do not the "educated" Negroes change their course by identifying themselves with the masses?

For similar reasons the Negro professional man may not always have a beautiful home and a fine car. His plight to the contrary may result from action like that of a poor man who

recently knocked on the author's door about
midnight to use his telephone to call the ambu-
lance of the Casualty Hospital to take immediate charge of his sick wife. Although living
nearer to the Freedmen's Hospital, where more
sympathetic consideration would have been
given this patient, he preferred to take her to
the other hospital where she would have to be
carried through the back yard and placed in a
room over a stable. He worked there, however; and because of long association with his
traducers and the sort of treatment that they
have meted out to him he was willing to entrust
to their hands the very delicate matter of the
health of his wife. This was a part of his community.

Large numbers of Negroes live in such a community. You say that such an atmosphere is
not congenial and you will not lose time with
these people who are thus satisfied, but the exploiting preacher, the unprincipled politician,
the notorious gambler, and the agent of vice are
all there purposely misleading these people who
have not as yet shaken from their minds the
shackles of slavery. What is going to become
of them? What is going to become of you?

We avoid them because we find enjoyment
among others; but they are developing their
own community. Their teacher lives in another
community which may or may not be growing.
Will his community so expand as to include

theirs? If not, their community may encroach upon his. It is a sort of social dualism. What will the end be? The teacher will help to answer this question.

Such guidance, however, must not be restricted to the so-called common people. So many Negroes now engaged in business have no knowledge of its possibilities and limitations. Most of them are as unwise as a Negro business man who came to Washington recently in a ten-thousand-dollar car representing a firm with only one hundred thousand dollars invested. It is only a matter of time before his firm will be no more. He started out destroying his business at the very source. While Negroes are thus spending their means and themselves in riotous living the foreigners come to dwell among them in modest circumstances long enough to get rich and to join those who close in on these unfortunates economically until all the hopes for their redemption are lost.

If the Negroes of this country are to escape starvation and rise out of poverty unto comfort and ease, they must change their way of thinking and living. Never did the author see a more striking demonstration of such a necessity than recently when a young man came to him looking for a job. He was well bedecked with jewelry and fine clothes, and while he was in the office he smoked almost enough cigars to pay one's board for that day. A man of this type in a poverty-stricken group must suffer and die.

A young woman recently displaced in a position from which she received considerable income for a number of years approached the author not long ago to help her solve the problem of making a living. He could not feel very sympathetic toward her, however, for she had on a coat which cost enough to maintain one comfortably for at least two years. While talking with him, moreover, she was so busy telling him about what she wanted that she had little time to inform him as to what she can do to supply her needs.

A man whom the author knows is decidedly handicapped by having lost a lucrative position. He must now work for a little more than half of what he has been accustomed to earn. With his former stipend he was able to maintain two or three girls in addition to his wife, and he drank the best of bootleg stuff available. In now trying to do all of these things on a small wage he finds himself following a most tortuous course to make his ends meet, and he suffers within as well as without.

This undesirable attitude toward life results from the fact that the Negro has learned from others how to spend money much more rapidly than he has learned how to earn it. During these days, therefore, it will be very wise for Negroes to concentrate on the wise use of money and the evil results from the misuse of it. In large cities like Washington, Baltimore, Philadelphia, New York, and Chicago they earn millions and millions every year and throw these vast sums immediately away for trifles which undermine their health, vitiate their morals, and contribute to the undoing of generations of Negroes unborn.

This enlightenment as to economic possibilities in the Negro community must not only include instruction as to how enterprises can be made possible but how they should be apportioned among the various parts of the Negro community. Such knowledge is especially necessary in the case of Negroes because of the fatal tendency toward imitation not only of the white man but the imitation of others in his own group. For example, a Negro starts a restaurant on a corner and does well. Another Negro, observing this prosperity, thinks that he can do just as well by opening a similar establishment next door. The inevitable result is that by dividing the trade between himself and his forerunner he makes it impossible for either one to secure sufficient patronage to continue in business.

In undertakings of great importance this same undesirable tendency toward duplication of effort is also apparent. It has been a common thing to find two or three banks in a Negro community, each one struggling for an existence in competing for the patronage of the small group of people, all of whom would hardly be able to support one such financial institution. These banks continue their unprofitable competition and never think of merging until some crisis forces them to the point that they have to do so or go into bankruptcy. The Negro community, then, never has a strong financial institution with sufficient resources to stimulate the efforts of the business men who otherwise might succeed.

The same shortsightedness has been evident in the case of the insurance companies organized by Negroes. One was established here and then another followed there in imitation of the first. We have been accustomed to boast that the Negroes have about fifty insurance companies in this country, marking the corners of the streets of the cities with large signs displaying what they are doing for the race. Instead of boasting of such unwise expansion we should have received such information with sorrow, for what the race actually needs is to merge all of the insurance companies now supported by Negroes and make one good one. Such a step away from duplication would be a long stride toward our much needed awakening, and it would certainly give us prestige in the business world.

This imitation and duplication are decidedly disastrous to economic enterprise as we can daily observe.. A few days ago a young man in the East lamented the fact that after investing his life's earnings in the drug business and making every effort to stimulate the enterprise, he has failed. Some one took occasion, thereupon, to remind him that men have grown rich, as a rule, not by doing what thousands of others are doing but by undertaking something new. If instead of going into the retail dispensing of drugs, he had conceived and carried out the idea of the chain-drug store, he would have become an independently rich man.

There is always a chance to do this because the large majority of people do not think and, therefore, leave the field wide open for those who have something new with which to please the public. Negroes even found this possible during the days of slavery when the race supposedly had no chance at all.

About a hundred years ago Thomas Day, a North Carolina Negro, realized that the rough furniture of the people in his community did not meet the requirements of those of modern taste. He, therefore, worked out a style of ornate and beautiful furniture which attracted the attention of the most aristocratic people of the state and built up for himself a most successful business. Persons in that state are still talking about the Day furniture, and not long ago it became the subject of a magazine article. If North Carolina would turn out more Negroes of this type today, instead of the rather large number who are going to teach and preach, some of its present economic problems might thereby be solved.

During these same years another Negro was showing himself to be equally ingenious. This was Henry Boyd. After buying himself in Kentucky, he went to Cincinnati to start life as a free man. There he encountered so much prejudice against Negro labor that he could not find employment at his trade of cabinetmaking. A new thought came to him, however; and in this way he solved his own problem.

Boyd became convinced that people had been sleeping long enough on straw ticks and wooden slats, and he invented the corded bed, the most comfortable bed prior to the use of springs which brought still more ease. Boyd's corded bed became popular throughout the Ohio and Mississippi Valleys, and he built up a profitable trade which required the employment of twenty-five white and black artisans. Other enterprising Negro business men like Boyd gave the Negro element of Cincinnati more of an aspect of progress before the Civil War than it has today. Has the Negro less chance today than he had a century ago?

For about thirty years the author knew an old Negro lady at Gordonsville, Virginia, who gave the world something new in frying chicken. She discovered the art of doing this thing in the

way that others could not, and she made a good
living selling her exceptionally prepared chicken
and fried puffs at the windows of the cars when
the trains stopped at the station. Well-to-do
men and women of both races would leave the
Pullman train with its modern diner attached
and go out and supply themselves and their
friends with this old lady's tastefully made up
lunches.

Another woman of color living in Columbia,
Missouri, recently gave the world another new
idea. She had learned cooking, especially bak-
ing, but saw no exceptional opportunity in the
usual application of the trade. After studying
her situation and the environment in which she
had to live, she hit upon the scheme of popularizing her savorous sweet potato biscuits,
beaten whiter than all others by an invention
of her own; and the people of both races made a
well-beaten path to her home to enjoy these
delicious biscuits. In this way she has made
herself and her relatives independent.

This is the way fortunes are made, but
Negroes, who are conscientiously doing their
best to rise in the economic sphere, do not follow the noble examples of those who had less
opportunity than we have today. We spend
much time in slavish imitation, but our white
friends strike out along new lines. Almost all
of the large fortunes in America have been made
in this way.

John D. Rockefeller did not set out in life to imitate Vanderbilt. Rockefeller saw his opportunity in developing the oil industry. Carnegie had better sense than to imitate Rockefeller, for that task was already well done, and he consolidated the steel interests. Henry Ford knew better than to take up what Carnegie had exploited, for there appeared a still larger possibility for industrial achievement in giving the world the facility of cheap transportation in the low-priced car.

While such guidance as the Negro needs will concern itself first with material things, however, it must not stop with these as ends in themselves. In the acquisition of these we lay the foundation for the greater things of the spirit. A poor man properly directed can write a more beautiful poem than one who is surfeited. The man in the hovel composes a more charming song than the one in the palace. The painter in the ghetto gets an inspiration for a more striking portrait than his landlord can appreciate. The ill-fed sculptor lives more abundantly than the millionaire who purchases the expression of his thought in marble and bronze. For the Negro, then, the door of opportunity is wide open. Let him prepare himself to enter this field where competition is no handicap. In such a sphere he may learn to lead the world, while keeping pace with it in the development of the material things of life.

CHAPTER XVI

NEGROES should study for the professions for all sane reasons that members of another race should go into these lines of endeavor and also on account of the particular call to serve the lowly of their race. In the case of the law we should cease to make exceptions because of the possibilities for failure resulting from prejudice against the Negro lawyer and the lack of Negro business enterprises to require his services. Negroes must become like English gentlemen who study the law of the land, not because they intend to practice the profession, but because every gentleman should know the law. In the interpretation of the law by the courts, too, all the rights of the Negroes in this country are involved; and a larger number of us must qualify for this important service. We may have too many lawyers of the wrong kind, but we have not our share of the right kind.

The Negro lawyer has tended to follow in the footsteps of the average white practitioner and has not developed the power which he could acquire if he knew more about the people whom he should serve and the problems they have to confront. These things are not law in themselves, but they determine largely whether or not the Negro will practice law and the success he will have in the profession. The failure to give attention to these things has often meant the downfall of many a Negro lawyer.

There are, moreover, certain aspects of law to which the white man would hardly address himself but to which the Negro should direct special attention. Of unusual importance to the Negro is the necessity for understanding the misrepresentations in criminal records of Negroes, and race distinctions in the laws of modern nations. These matters require a systematic study of the principles of law and legal procedure and, in addition thereto, further study of legal problems as they meet the Negro lawyer in the life which he must live. This offers the Negro law school an unusual opportunity.

Because our lawyers do not give attention to these problems they often fail in a crisis. They are interested in the race and want to defend its cause. The case, however, requires not only the unselfish spirit they sometimes manifest but much more understanding of the legal principles involved. Nothing illustrates this better than the failure of one of our attorneys to measure up in the case brought up to the United States Supreme Court from Oklahoma to test the validity of the exclusion of Negroes from Pullman cars. The same criticism may be made of the segregation case of the District of Columbia brought before this highest tribunal by another Negro attorney. In both of these cases the lawyers started wrong and therefore ended wrong. They lacked the knowledge to present their cases properly to the court.

Our lawyers must learn that the judges are not attorneys themselves, for they have to decide on the merits of what is presented to them. It is not the business of the judges to amend their pleadings or decide their cases according to their good intentions. Certainly such generosity cannot be expected from prejudiced courts which are looking for every loophole possible to escape from a frank decision on the rights of Negroes guaranteed by the constitution. These matters require advanced study and painstaking research; but our lawyers, as a rule, are not interested in this sort of mental exercise.

The Negro medical schools have had a much better opportunity than the few Negro law schools which have functioned in the professional preparation of Negroes. On account of the racial contact required of white physicians who are sometimes unwilling to sustain this relation to Negroes the Negro physicians and dentists have a better chance among their people than the Negro lawyers; and the demand for the services of the former assures a larger income than Negro lawyers are accustomed to earn. But in spite of this better opportunity Negro medical institutions and their graduates have done little more than others to solve the peculiar problems confronting the Negro race.

Too many Negroes go into medicine and dentistry merely for selfish purposes, hoping thereby to increase their income and spend it in joyous living. They have the ambition to own fine automobiles, to dress handsomely, and to figure conspicuously in society. The practice of these professions among poor Negroes yields these results. Why not be a physician or dentist then?

Too many of our physicians are like the one whom the author recently visited in New York City. "When I heard you coming up the stairs," said he, "I began to feel glad, for I was sure that you were another patient from whom I might extract at least two dollars for a prescription."

Yet one would wonder how that physician could prosper in his profession, for he had no special equipment for the practice of any kind of advanced phases of medicine. About all he could do was to look at the patient's tongue, feel his pulse, ask him a few questions, write a prescription and collect the fee. The apparatus required for the modern treatment of serious maladies he did not have and seemed to have no ambition to possess.

The Negroes of today are very much in need of physicians who in their professional work will live up to what they are taught in school, and will build upon their foundation by both experience and further training. In his segregated position in the ghetto the Negro health problem presents more difficulties than that of the whites who are otherwise circumstanced. The longevity of the Negro depends in part upon the supply of Negro physicians and nurses who will address themselves unselfishly to the solution of this particular problem. Since the Negroes are forced into undesirable situations and compelled to inhabit germ-infested districts, they cannot escape ultimate extermination if our physicians do not help them to work out a community health program which will provide for the Negroes some way to survive.

Negro medical schools and their graduates must do more preaching of the necessity for improving conditions which determine health and eradicate disease. A large number of physicians and nurses must be trained, and new opportunities for them to practice must be found. This can be done by turning out better products from these schools and the extension of hospitals among Negroes who have been so long neglected. In this campaign, however, the Negro physicians must supply the leadership, and others must join with them in these efforts.

From medical schools, too, we must have

Negroes with a program of medical research.
Today the world is inclined to give attention to
the health of the Negro since unsanitary conditions of the race will mean the loss of health
among the whites. Philanthropists, however,
hardly know how to proceed or which way
to go because they have so long neglected the
Negroes that they do not know how to provide
wisely for them; and the Negro physicians
themselves have failed to give adequate attention to these conditions. Negro medical students
have not directed sufficient attention to the ante-
bellum background of the Negro who, still under
that influence, indulges in superstitious and religious practices which impede the progress of
medicine among them. One would be surprised
to know the extent to which primitive medicine
is practiced among American Negroes today.
Often in the rural districts they seldom see a
physician. The midwife and the herb doctor
there control the situation.

The greatest problem now awaiting solution
is the investigation of the differential resistance
of races to disease. What are the diseases
of which Negroes are more susceptible than
whites? What are the diseases of which the
whites are more susceptible than Negroes? The
Negro escapes yellow fever and influenza, but
the white man dies. The white man withstands
syphilis and tuberculosis fairly well, but the
Negro afflicted with these maladies easily suc-

cumbs. These questions offer an inviting field of research for Negro medical students.

While we hear much about medicine, law and the like their importance must not be unduly emphasized. Certainly men should not crowd into these spheres to make money, but all professions among Negroes except those of teaching and preaching are undermanned. All Negroes in professions constitute less than two and a half per cent of those over ten years of age who are gainfully employed. At the same time the whites find certain of their professions overcrowded, and some of their practitioners could not exist without the patronage of Negroes.

Negroes, too, should undergo systematic training for those professions in which they have shown special aptitude as in the arts. They must not wait for the Americans to approve their plunging into unknown spheres. The world is not circumscribed by the United States, and the Negro must become a pioneer in making use of a larger portion of the universe. If the people here do recognize the Negro in these spheres let him seek a hearing in the liberal circles of Europe. If he has any art Europeans will appreciate it and assure him success in forbidden fields.

In Europe, it should be noted, the Negro artist is not wanted as a mere imitator. Europeans will recognize him in the rôle of an enlightened

179

artist portraying the life of his people. As an English abolitionist said more than a century ago, "The portrait of the Negro has seldom been drawn but by the pencil of his oppressor and the Negro has sat for it in the distorted attitude of slavery." A new method of approach, however, is now possible. There has been an awakening in Europe to the realization of the significance of African culture, and circles there want to see that life depicted by the Negro who can view it from within. There is a philosophy in it that the world must understand. From its contemplation may come a new social program. Herein lies the opportunity of the Negro artist as a world reformer. Will he see it and live or continue the mere imitation of others and die?

CHAPTER XVII

ANOTHER factor the Negro needs is a new figure in politics, one who will not concern himself so much with what others can do for him as with what he can do for himself. He will know sufficient about the system of government not to carry his trouble to the federal functionaries and thus confess himself a failure in the community in which he lives. He will know that his freedom from peonage and lynching will be determined by the extent that he can develop into a worthy citizen and impress himself upon his community.

The New Negro in politics will not be so unwise as to join the ignorant delegations from conferences and conventions which stage annual pilgrimages to the White House to complain to the President because they have socially and economically failed to measure up to demands of self-preservation. The New Negro in politics will understand clearly that in the final analysis federal functionaries cannot do anything about these matters within the police powers of the states, and he will not put himself in the position of being received with coldness and treated with contempt as these ignorant misleaders of the Negro race have been from time immemorial. The New Negro in politics, then, will appeal to his own and to such friends of other races in his locality as believe in social justice. If he does something for himself others will do more for him.

The increasing vigor of the race, then, will not be frittered away in partisan strife in the interest of the oppressors of the race. It ought not to be possible for the political bosses to induce almost any Negro in the community to abandon his permanent employment to assist them and their ilk in carrying out some program for the selfish purposes of the ones engineering the scheme. It ought not to be possible for the politicians to distribute funds at the rate of fifty or a hundred dollars a head among the outstanding ministers and use them and their congregations in vicious partisan strife. It is most shameful that some ministers resort to religion as a camouflage to gain influence in the churches only to use such power for selfish political purpose.

The Negro should endeavor to be a figure in politics, not a tool for the politicians. This higher rôle can be played not by parking all of the votes of a race on one side of the fence as both blacks and whites have done in the South, but by independent action. The Negro should not censure the Republican party for forgetting him and he should not blame the Democratic party for opposing him. Neither can the South blame any one but itself for its isolation in national politics. Any people who will vote the same way for three generations without thereby obtaining results ought to be ignored and disfranchised.

As a minority element the Negro should not knock at the door of any particular political party. He should appeal to the Negroes themselves and from them should come harmony and concerted action for a new advance to that larger freedom of men. The Negro should use his vote rather than give it away to reward the dead for some favors done in the distant past. He should clamor not for the few offices earmarked as Negro jobs but for the recognition of these despised persons as men according to the provision of the Constitution of the United States.

The few state and national offices formerly set aside for Negroes have paled into insignificance when compared with the many highly lucrative positions now occupied by Negroes as a result of their development in other spheres. Sometimes a Negro prominent in education, business or professional life can earn more in a few months than the most successful politicians can earn in years. These political jobs, moreover, have diminished in recent years because the increase of race prejudice, which this policy has doubtless aided, supplies the political leaders with an excuse for not granting their Negro coworkers anything additional.

The New Negro in politics must learn something that the old "ward-heelers" have never been able to realize, namely, not only that the few offices allotted Negroes are insignificant but that even if the Negro received a proportionate share of the spoils, the race cannot hope to solve any serious problem by the changing fortunes of politics. Real politics, the science of government, is deeply rooted in the economic foundation of the social order. To figure greatly in politics the Negro must be a great figure in politics. A class of people slightly lifted above poverty, therefore, can never have much influence in political circles. The Negro must develop character and worth to make him a desirable everywhere so that he will not have to knock at the doors of political parties but will have them thrown open to him.

The New Negro in politics must not ask the party for money, he must not hire himself for a pittance to swing voters in line. He must contribute to the campaign of the party pleasing him, rather than draw upon it for an allowance to drive the wolf from the door during the three months of the political canvass. It will be considered a stroke of good fortune that a Negro of such influence and character has aligned himself with a party, and this fact will speak eloquently for the element to which he belongs.

The New Negro in politics, moreover, must not be a politician. He must be a man. He must try to give the world something rather than extract something from it. The world, as he should see it, does not owe him anything, certainly not a political office; and he should not try solely to secure one, and thus waste valuable years which might be devoted to the development of something of an enduring value. If he goes into office, it should be as a sacrifice, because his valuable time is required elsewhere. If he is needed by his country in a civil position, he may respond to the call as a matter of duty, for his usefulness is otherwise assured. From such a Negro, then, we may expect sound advice, intelligent guidance, and constructive effort for the good of all elements of our population.

When such Negroes go into office you will not find them specializing in things which peculiarly concern the Negroes, offering merely anti-lynching bills and measures for pensioning the freedmen. The New Negro in politics will see his opportunity not in thus restricting himself but in visioning the whole social and economic order with his race as a part of it. In thus working for the benefit of all as prompted by his liberal mindedness the New Negro will do much more to bring the elements together for common good than he will be able to do in prating only of the ills of his particular corner and extending his hand for a *douceur*.

In suggesting herein the rise of the New Negro in politics the author does not have in mind the so-called radical Negroes who have read and misunderstood Karl Marx and his disciples and would solve the political as well as the economic problems of the race by an immediate application of these principles. History shows that although large numbers of people have actually tried to realize such pleasant dreams, they have in the final analysis come back to a social program based on competition. If no one is to enjoy the fruits of his exceptional labor any more than the individual who is not prepared to render such extraordinary service, not one of a thousand will be sufficiently humanitarian to bestir himself to achieve much of importance, and force applied in this case to stimulate such action has always broken down. If the excited whites who are bringing to the Negroes such strange doctrines are insane enough to believe them, the Negroes themselves should learn to think before it is too late.

History shows that it does not matter who is in power or what revolutionary forces take over the government, those who have not learned to do for themselves and have to depend solely on others never obtain any more rights or privileges in the end than they had in the beginning. Even if the expected social upheaval comes, the Negro will be better prepared to take care of himself in the subsequent reconstruction if he develops the power to ascend to a position higher up after the radically democratic people will have recovered from their revelry in an impossible Utopia.

To say that the Negro cannot develop sufficiently in the business world to measure arms with present-day capitalists is to deny actual facts, refute history, and discredit the Negro as a capable competitor in the economic battle of life. No man knows what he can do until he tries. The Negro race has never tried to do very much for itself. The race has great possibilities. Properly awakened, the Negro can do the so-called impossible in the business world and thus help to govern rather than merely be governed.

In the failure to see this and the advocacy of the destruction of the whole economic order to right social wrong we see again the tendency of the Negro to look to some force from without to do for him what he must learn to do for himself. The Negro needs to become radical, and the race will never amount to anything until it does become so, but this radicalism should come from within. The Negro will be very foolish to resort to extreme measures in behalf of foreign movements before he learns to suffer and die to right his own wrongs. There is no movement in the world working especially for the Negro. He must learn to do this for himself or be exterminated just as the American Indian has faced his doom in the setting sun.

Why should the Negro wait for some one from without to urge him to self-assertion when he sees himself robbed by his employer, defrauded by his merchant, and hushed up by government agents of injustice? Why wait for a spur to action when he finds his manhood insulted, his women outraged, and his fellowmen lynched for amusement? The Negroes have always had sufficient reason for being radical, and it looks silly to see them taking up the cause of others who pretend that they are interested in the Negro when they merely mean to use the race as a means to an end. When the desired purpose of these so-called friendly groups will have been served, they will have no further use for the Negro and will drop him just as the Republican machine has done.

The radicals bring forward, too, the argument that the Negro, being of a minority group, will always be overpowered by others. From the point of view of the selfish elements this may be true, and certainly it has worked thus for some time; but things do not always turn out according to mathematical calculations. In fact, the significant developments in history have never been thus determined. Only the temporary and the trivial can be thus forecast.

The human factor is always difficult for the materialist to evaluate and the prophecies of the alarmist are often upset. Why should we expect less in the case of the Negro?

CHAPTER XVIII

THE STUDY OF THE NEGRO

The facts drawn from an experience of more than twenty years enable us to make certain deductions with respect to the study of the Negro. Only one Negro out of every ten thousand is interested in the effort to set forth what his race has thought and felt and attempted and accomplished that it may not become a negligible factor in the thought of the world. By traditions and education, however, the large majority of Negroes have become interested in the history and status of other races, and they spend millions annually to promote such knowledge. Along with this sum, of course, should be considered the large amount paid for devices in trying not to be Negroes.

The chief reason why so many give such a little attention to the background of the Negro is the belief that this study is unimportant. They consider as history only such deeds as those of Mussolini who after building up an efficient war machine with the aid of other Europeans would now use it to murder unarmed and defenseless Africans who have restricted themselves exclusively to attending to their own business. If Mussolini succeeds in crushing Abyssinia he will be recorded in "history" among the Caesars, and volumes written in praise of the conqueror will find their way to the homes and libraries of thousands of mis-educated Negroes. The oppressor has always indoctrinated the weak with this interpretation of the crimes of the strong.

The war lords have done good only accidentally or incidentally while seeking to do evil. The movements which have ameliorated the condition of humanity and stimulated progress have been inaugurated by men of thought in lifting their fellows out of drudgery unto ease and comfort, out of selfishness unto altruism. The Negro may well rejoice that his hands, unlike those of his opporessors, are not stained with so much blood extracted by brute force. Real history is not the record of the successes and disappointments, the vices, the follies, and the quarrels of those who engage in contention for power.

The Association for the Study of Negro Life and History is projected on the fact that there is nothing in the past of the Negro more shameful than what is found in the past of other races. The Negro is as human as the other members of the family of mankind. The Negro, like others, has been up at times; and at times he has been down. With the domestication of animals, the discovery of iron, the development of stringed instruments, an advancement in fine art, and the inauguration of trial by jury to his credit, the Negro stands just as high as others in contributing to the progress of the world.

The oppressor, however, raises his voice to the contrary. He teaches the Negro that he has no worth-while past, that his race has done nothing significant since the beginning of time, and that there is no evidence that he will ever achieve anything great. The education of the Negro then must be carefully directed lest the race may waste time trying to do the impossible. Lead the Negro to believe this and thus control his thinking. If you can thereby determine what he will think, you will not need to worry about what he will do. You will not have to tell him to go to the back door. He will go without being told; and if there is no back door he will have one cut for his special benefit.

If you teach the Negro that he has accomplished as much good as any other race he will aspire to equality and justice without regard to race. Such an effort would upset the program of the oppressor in Africa and America. Play up before the Negro, then, his crimes and shortcomings. Let him learn to admire the Hebrew, the Greek, the Latin and the Teuton. Lead the Negro to detest the man of African blood—to hate himself. The oppressor then may conquer exploit, oppress and even annihilate the Negro by segregation without fear or trembling. With the truth hidden there will be little expression of thought to the contrary.

The American Negro has taken over an abundance of information which others have made accessible to the oppressed, but he has not yet learned to think and plan for himself as others do for themselves. Well might this race be referred to as the most docile and tractable people on earth. This merely means that when the oppressors once start the large majority of the race in the direction of serving the purposes of their traducers, the task becomes so easy in the years following that they have little trouble with the masses thus controlled. It is a most satifactory system, and it has become so popular that European nations of foresight are sending some of their brightest minds to the United States to observe the Negro in "inaction" in order to learn how to deal likewise with Negroes in their colonies. What the Negro in America has become satisfied with will be accepted as the measure of what should be allotted him elsewhere. Certain Europeans consider the "solution of the race problem in the United States" one of our great achievements.

The mis-educated Negro joins the opposition with the objection that the study of the Negro keeps alive questions which should be forgotten. The Negro should cease to remember that he was once held a slave, that he has been oppressed, and even that he is a Negro. The traducer, however, keeps before the public such aspects of this history as will justify the present oppression of the race. It would seem, then, that the Negro should emphasize at the same time the favorable aspects to justify action in his behalf. One cannot blame the Negro for not desiring to be reminded of being the sort of creature that the oppressor has represented the Negro to be; but this very attitude shows ignorance of the past and a slavish dependence upon the enemy to serve those whom he would destroy. The Negro can be made proud of his past only by approaching it scientifically himself and giving his own story to the world. What others have written about the Negro during the last three centuries has been mainly for the purpose of bringing him where he is today and holding him there.

The method employed by the Association for the Study of Negro Life and History, however, is not spectacular propanganda or fire-eating agitation. Nothing can be accomplished in such fashion. "Whom the gods would destroy they first make mad." The Negro, whether in Africa or America, must be directed toward a serious examination of the fundamentals of education, religion, literature, and philosophy as they have been expounded to him. He must be sufficiently enlightened to determine for himself whether these forces have come into his life to bless him or to bless his oppressor. After learning the facts in the case the Negro must develop the power of execution to deal with these matters as do people of vision. Problems of great importance cannot be worked out in a day. Questions of great moment must be met with far-reaching plans.

The Association for the Study of Negro Life and History is teaching the Negro to exercise foresight rather than "hindsight." Liberia must not wait until she is offered to Germany before realizing that she has few friends in Europe. Abyssinia must not wait until she is invaded by Italy before she prepares for self-defense. A scientific study of the past of modern nations would show these selfish tendencies as inevitable results from their policies in dealing with those whom they have professed to elevate. For example, much of Africa has been conquered and subjugated to save souls. How expensive has been the Negro's salvation! One of the strong arguments for slavery was that it brought the Negro into the light of salvation. And yet the Negro today is all but lost.

The Association for the Study of Negro Life and History, however, has no special brand for the solution of the race problem except to learn to think. No general program of uplift for the Negroes in all parts of the world will be any more successful than such a procedure would be in the case of members of other races under different circumstances. What will help a Negro in Alabama may prove harmful to one in Maine. The African Negro may find his progress retarded by applying "methods used for the elevation of the Negro in America." A thinking man, however, learns to deal wisely with conditions as he finds them rather than to take orders from some one who knows nothing about his status and cares less. At present the Negro, both in Africa and America, is being turned first here and there experimentally by so-called friends who in the final analysis assist the Negro merely in remaining in the dark.

In the furtherance of the program of taking up these matters dispassionately the Association had made available an outline for the systematic study of the Negro as he has touched the life of others and as others have functioned in their relation to him, *The African Background Outlined: A Handbook*. This book is written from the point of view of history, literature, art, education, religion and economic imperialism. In seventeen chapters as Part I of the work a brief summary of the past in Africa is presented; and courses on "The Negro in Africa," "The Negro in the European Mind," "The Negro in America," "The Negro in Literature," "The Negro in Art," "The Education of the Negro," "The Religious Development of the Negro," and "Economic Imperialism," follow as Part II with ample bibliographical comment for every heading and subhead of these outlines. This facilitates the task of clubs, young peoples' societies, and special classes organized where the oppressors of the race and the Negroes cooperating with them are determined that the history and status of the Negro shall not be made a part of the curricula.

In this outline there is no animus, nothing to engender race hate. The Association does not bring out such publications. The aim of this organization is to set forth facts in scientific form, for facts properly set forth will tell their own story. No advantage can be gained by merely inflaming the Negro's mind against his traducers. In a manner they deserve to be congratulated for taking care of their own interests so well. The Negro needs to become angry with himself because he has not handled his own affairs wisely. In other words, the Negro must learn from others how to take care of himself in this trying ordeal. He must not remain content with taking over what others set aside for him and then come in the guise of friends to subject even that limited information to further misinterpretation.

APPENDIX

MUCH ADO ABOUT A NAME

A PARTICIPANT who recently attended an historical meeting desired to take up the question as to what the race should be called. *Africans, Negroes, colored people,* or what? This is a matter of much concern to him because he hopes thereby to solve the race problem. If others will agree to call Negroes Nordics, he thinks, he will reach the desired end by taking a short cut.

This may sound all but insane, but there are a good many "highly educated" Negroes who believe that such can be accomplished by this shift in terminology; and they have spent time and energy in trying to effect a change. Many of this class suffer mentally because of the frequent use of "offensive expressions" in addressing Negroes. When dealing with them, then, one has to be very careful. For this reason our friends in other races have to seek guidance in approaching us. For example, Lady Simon, the wife of Sir John Simon of the British Cabinet, has recently asked an American Negro what his people prefer to be called; and later in England she took up the same matter with another member of this race. Being an advocate of freedom, she has written considerably to advance its cause. She would not like to use in her works, then, an expression which may hurt some one's feelings.

Although a student of social problems, this learned woman cannot fathom this peculiar psychology. Americans, too, must confess the difficulty of understanding it, unless it is that the "highly educated

Negro mind'' tends to concern itself with trifles rather than with the great problems of life. We have known Negroes to ask for a separate Y. M. C. A. or Y. W. C. A., a separate church or a separate school, and then object to calling the institution *colored* or *Negro*. These segregationists have compromised on principle, but they are unwilling to acknowledge their crime against justice. The name, they believe, will save them from the disgrace.

It does not matter so much what the thing is called as what the thing is. The Negro would not cease to be what he is by calling him something else; but, if he will struggle and make something of himself and contribute to modern culture, the world will learn to look upon him as an American rather than as one of an undeveloped element of the population.

The word *Negro* or *black* is used in referring to this particular element because most persons of native African descent approach this color. The term does not imply that every Negro is black; and the word white does not mean that every white man is actually white. Negroes may be *colored,* but many Caucasians are scientifically classified as *colored.* We are not all Africans, moreover, because many of us were not born in Africa; and we are not all Afro-Americans, because few of us are natives of Africa transplanted to America.

There is nothing to be gained by running away from the name. The names of practically all races and nations at times have connoted insignificance and low social status. Angles and Saxons, once the slaves of Romans, experienced this; and even the name of the Greek for a while meant no more than this to these conquerors of the world. The people who bore these names, however, have made them grand and illustrious. The Negro must learn to do the same.

It is strange, too, that while the Negro feels ashamed

of his name, persons abroad do not usually think of it in this sense. One does find in Europe a number of West Indian and American Negroes of some Caucasian blood, who do not want to be known as Negroes. As a rule, however, a European of African Negro blood feels proud of this racial heritage and delights to be referred to as such. The writer saw a striking case of this in London in the granddaughter of a Zulu chief. She is so far removed from the African type that one could easily mistake her for a Spaniard; and yet she thinks only for her African connection and gets her inspiration mainly from the story of her people beyond the Pillars of Hercules.

The writer was agreeably surprised a few days later, too, when he met a prominent Parisian with the same attitude. He has produced several volumes in which he champions the cause of the Negro because he has in his veins the same blood. A well-to-do European woman, the daughter of a Dutchman and an African mother, is similarly enthusiastic over her Negro blood. The first thing she mentioned in conversing with the writer was that black mother. This young woman expressed the regret that she did not have more of that color that she, too, might say, as do members of certain tribes of Africa: "I am black and comely. I am black and beautiful. I am beautifully black."

These people surprise you when you think of the attitude of many American Negroes on this question. These race-conscious people can think, but it is seldom that the American Negro indulges in such an exercise. He has permitted other people to determine for him the attitude that he has toward his own people. This means the enslavement of his mind and eventually the enslavement of his body.

Some Europeans rather regard the word Negro as romantic. Going now along the streets of Paris, one will see advertised such places as "l'Elan Noir," and the "Café au Nègre de Toulouse." In one of these cases the writer was especially attracted by the "Choppe du Nègre" and took dinner there one day. The cuisine was excellent, the music rendered by the orchestra was charming, and a jolly crowd came to enjoy themselves. However, he was the only "Nègre" there.

Walking along a street in Geneva not long ago, the writer's attention was attracted to something of the sort, which is still more significant. It was a wholesale coffee house called "A La Case de l'Oncle Tom." He entered and asked: "Why did you give this store such a name?" The proprietress laughed and explained that her grandfather, François Prudhom, who had read "Uncle Tom's Cabin" and had been deeply impressed thereby, selected this name for the store when he established it in 1866.

THE VALUE OF COLOR

NOT long ago the writer saw on a street car one of the prettiest women in the world. She was a perfectly black woman becomingly dressed in suitable gray and modest adornments which harmonized with her color. She was naturally a commanding figure without any effort to please others, for her bearing was such that she would not fail to attract attention. He could not restrain myself from gazing at her; and, looking around to see whether others were similarly concerned, he found the whites in the car admiring her also, even to the point of commenting among themselves.

This woman's common sense, manifested in knowing how to dress, had made her color an asset rather than a liability. The writer easily recalled, then, that tribe in Africa that feels unusually proud of being black. We are told that they are so anxious to be black that if they find one of the group with a tendency to depart the least from this color they go to the heart of nature and extract from it its darkest dye and paint therewith that native's face that he may continue perfectly black.

Here in America, however, we are ashamed of being black. So many of us who are actually black powder our faces and make ourselves blue. In so doing we become all but hideous by the slavish aping of those around us in keeping with our custom of imitation. We fail to take ourselves for what we are actually worth, and do not make the most of ourselves.

We show lack of taste in the selection of our dress. We long for what others wear whether it harmonizes with our color or not. They have given particular attention to design with respect to their race and have written books to this effect. Thinking, however, that the Negro is not supposed to wear anything but what the poor may pick up, the artists have not thought seriously of him. Both teachers and students of nearby schools thus concerned, then, repeatedly appeal to us for help in the study of design with respect to the Negro, but we have nothing scientific to offer them. We have no staff of artists who can function in this sphere.

To be able to supply this need requires the most painstaking effort to understand colors and color schemes. It is a very difficult task because of the variation of color within the race. Sometimes in one family of ten you will hardly find two of the same shade. To dress them all alike may be economical, but the world thereby misses that much of beauty. The Negro mother, then, needs to be the real artist, and the schools now training the youth to be the parents of tomorrow should give as much attention to these things esthetic as they do to language, literature or mathematics.

In neglecting to know himself better from this point of view, then, the Negro is making a costly mistake. He should be deeply concerned with the esthetic possibilities of his situation. In this so-called Negro race we have the prettiest people in the world, when they dress in harmony with the many shades and colors with which we are so richly endowed. Why do we go away from home to find what we already have on hand?

Recently one saw in Washington a demonstration of the value of color when the Masonic conclave staged a tremendous parade in this national city. The whites were attracted to the upstanding, outstanding Negroes so becomingly bedecked in costumes of the Orient. This, however, was accidental. The color of the Negroes happened to be Oriental, and the colors of this order were originally worked out to suit the people of those parts. The dead white of the Caucasian does not harmonize with such garb. Why, then should the Negro worry about what others wear?

Carrying the imitation of others to an extreme to-day, we do not find ourselves far in advance of the oppressed antebellum Negroes, who, unable to dress themselves, had to take whatever others threw at them. We make a most hideous spectacle, then, when we are on dress parade in our social atmosphere. So many of us clad in unbecoming colors often look like decorated pet horses turned loose for an hour or so of freedom.

Appreciating the value of color, the artists in European cities are trying to change their hue to that of the colored people. They can understand how inexpressive the dead white is, and they are trying to make use of what we are seeking to conceal. The models in their shops are purposely colored to display to good effect the beautiful costumes which require color.

Some of these Europeans frankly tell Negroes how they envy them for their color.

One is not surprised, then, to find European cafés and hotels employing American or African Negroes to supply this color which the Europeans lack. Pictures of such black men are sometimes displayed to great effect. That of Josephine Baker adorns the windows of large stores in Paris. Here in America, too, we observe that art centres are likewise getting away from the dead white to enjoy the richness of color.

The writer felt somewhat encouraged recently when he talked with a Washington lady who runs "The Pandora," a unique establishment devoted to design. Upon inquiring about her progress in the effort to teach colored people how to wear what becomes them, she reported considerable success. Sometimes customers insist on purchasing unbecoming attire, but usually she has shown them the unwisdom of so doing, and most of them now take her advice.

In this way this enterprising woman is not only conducting a pioneer business, but she is rendering a social service. She has not had any special training in this work, but on her initiative she is building upon what she has learned by studying the Negroes in her community. Others of us may do likewise, if we try to help the Negro rather than exploit him.

INDEX

INDEX

210

North, aid given by, to Negro education in South, 12, 26

North Carolina, teaching of Negro history in, 135

Northern Negro, hostility of, toward Southern Negro, 97-98

Northern, white Southerner, interest of, in Negro education, 26

Northern institutions, 3

O

Ovid, quotation from, 111

P

"Pandora, The," house of design, 197

Paul, Nathaniel, opposition of, to colonization, 98; opposition of, to slavery, 99

Peonage, a result of false education, xii

Perry, Commodore, on Lake Erie, reference to, 155

Philosophy, few contributions to, by American Negroes, 15; contributions to, by Africans, 137

Physicians, insufficient number of, 75; display by, 124-125, 176; better preparation of, 175-176; exploitation by, 176

Pittsburgh, objectionable terms in school books of, 141-142

Police powers of States, importance of, 181-182

Political education, neglect of, 84-95

Politics, Negroes in, during Reconstruction, 10-11; disfranchisement of Negroes in, 88-90; corruption of Negroes in, 90-93, 182; restricted rôle of Negroes in, 92-94; mistakes of Negroe in, 94; contributions of Negroes in, 94-95; new pro-

gram in, 181-189; Negroes as tools in, 182-183; loss of Negro jobs in, 183-184

Professions, decline of Negro in, 24; mis-education for, 74-82; discouragement from entering, 75-76; new program in, 173-180; overcrowding in, 179. See also Law, Medicine, Negro Ministers.

Proverbs, African, philosophy in, 150

Psychology of the Negro, ignorance of, by Negroes, 5; knowledge of, by whites, 5

Public schools, establishment of, during Reconstruction, 11; failure of, in Negro education, 11

Purvis, Robert, opposition of, to colonization, 98

Pushkin, reference to, 15

R

Race, as a factor in education, xi-xii, 17

Racial attitudes, difficulty of changing, after adolescence, 135-136

Radicalism, necessity for proper kind of, 187-188

Real estate, unprincipled Negroes in, 105

Reconstruction, political power of Negroes in, 11; schools established during, 11, rôle of Negroes in, 94-95, 96

Religion, false teachings of, xii, 59-60; borrowed from whites, 57-58, 61; need for change in, 145-148

Remond, Charles L., fearless attack of, on Jim-Crowism, 99-100

Ritualistic churches, little appeal in, for Negro masses, 55

SEVEN COMMENTS ON THE MIS-EDUCATION OF THE NEGRO

I. Here we have a Negro's presentation of the problems which attend the education of the colored people at the careless or misguided hands of white men. Here is one who has found that his degrees earned from leading white universities have ill-fitted him for leading his people out of ignorance and prejudice to a place in the sun to which they may be ultimately entitled by virtue of inherent, altho undeveloped capacity.—*The Syracuse Post-Standard*

II. Mr. Woodson's book is deserving of much commendation because it is fearless and constructive and directed toward a closer understanding of the one problem that America has been unable successfully to solve.—*Sunday Times-Advertiser (Trenton)*

III. This is a challenging book. It throws down the gauntlet to those who have had anything to do with Negro education, whether of white or black race, and it bids the Negro to come forward in pride of race and heritage and, standing on the basis of his own racial personality, demand an education that will develop that personality and its gifts rather than seek merely to imitate the white.—*The New York Times*

IV. The course of study as outlined by the ruling class preaches the inferiority of the Negro and dismisses any achievement with a shrug of shoulders or a wave of the hand. In the economic classes one learns that the Negro cannot be successful as a business man; in the history class he is pictured as a human being of the lowest order; and likewise in all other subjects he is belittled or omitted. Therefore, contends Dr. Woodson, the entire system must be reconstructed if it is to be of any use to Negroes in their process of development.—*The Amsterdam News*

V. Not only has the white American been educated to regard the Negro as inferior, but the thinking of the Negro himself has been influenced through school and college so that he regards himself as inferior. His racial virtues and achievements and possibilities are disregarded, and not known or understood as they should be by either white or Negro educators or educated. This book is a challenge and a protest against the white American tradition and system of education, with all its hypocrisy and prejudice, its injustice and inadequacy. It also reminds us

that the Negro who thinks today is in revolt, as he should be.—
The Congregationalist

VI. He sounds a protest against the type of instruction received by
the Negro, by calling attention to the old culture, literature and
art of the native Africans. He tells of Negro empires rivaling
Rome in their power. Yet such matters are omitted from all our
textbooks, both for whites and blacks. Instead, they pass by
Africa and its inhabitants and leave a negative impression in
the mind of the student. Woodson argues that the universities
founded for his race breed contempt for the blacks. More often
than not, these schools are run by white men, who by various
actions impress upon the students a feeling of racial inequality.
—*Columbia Missourian*

VII. This mis-education of the Negro teaches him to slavishly imitate
the white rather than to develop his racial gifts, forgetting that
"History does not furnish a case of the elevation of a people
by ignoring the thought and aspiration of a people thus served."
—*The Salt Lake Tribune*